INSTITUTE OF LEADERSHIP & MANAGEMENT **ilm**

SUPER**SERIES**

Collecting Information

FOURTH EDITION

LEARNING RESOURCES
CENTRE

Havering College
of Further and Higher Education

Published for the
Institute of Leadership & Management by

Pergamon
Flexible
Learning

OXFORD   AMSTERDAM   BOSTON   LONDON   NEW YORK   PARIS
SAN DIEGO   SAN FRANCISCO   SINGAPORE   SYDNEY   TOKYO

Pergamon Flexible Learning
An imprint of Elsevier
Linacre House, Jordan Hill, Oxford OX2 8DP
30 Corporate Drive, Burlington, MA 01803

First published 1986
Second edition 1991
Third edition 1997
Fourth edition 2003
Reprinted 2005

British Library Cataloguing in Publication Data
A catalogue record for this book is available from the British Library

ISBN 0 7506 5888 6

For information on Pergamon Flexible Learning
visit our website at www.bh.com/pergamonfl

Institute of Leadership & Management
registered office
1 Giltspur Street
London
EC1A 9DD
Telephone 020 7294 3053
www.i-l-m.com
ILM is part of the City & Guilds Group

Working together to grow
libraries in developing countries

www.elsevier.com | www.bookaid.org | www.sabre.org

ELSEVIER   BOOK AID
            International   Sabre Foundation

The views expressed in this work are those of the authors and do
not necessarily reflect those of the Institute of Leadership &
Management or of the publisher

Crown Copyright material is reproduced with the permission of
the Controller of HMSO and the Queen's Printer for Scotland

Author: Bob Foley
With additional material by Heather Serjeant
Editor: Bob Foley
Partially based on previous material by Howard Senter
Editorial management: Genesys, www.genesys-consultants.com
Composition by Genesis Typesetting Limited, Rochester, Kent
Printed and bound in Great Britain by MPG Books, Bodmin

Contents

Contents

Workbook introduction

1 ILM Super Series study links

This workbook addresses the issues of *Collecting Information*. Should you wish to extend your study to other Super Series workbooks covering related or different subject areas, you will find a comprehensive list at the back of this book.

2 Links to ILM Qualifications

This workbook relates to the following learning outcomes in segments from the ILM Level 3 Introductory Certificate in First Line Management and the Level 3 Certificate in First Line Management.

C10.1   Gathering valid information
  1   Understand the need for information
  2   Identify means of collecting and recording data and/or information
  3   Gather information relevant to own area of responsibility
  4   Recognize any constraints on the collection of, and access to, data
  5   Check sources and validity of data

C10.6   IT applications
  1   Identify the use and application of spreadsheets and databases
  2   Explain the value of electronic communication methods

C10.7 Sources of information
1 Identify a range of information sources which may be used in the organization
2 Explain the use and value of internal sources
3 Explain the nature and use of external sources
4 Explain how the Internet may be accessed and used as an information resource

3 Links to S/NVQs in Management

This workbook relates to the following elements of the Management Standards which are used in S/NVQs in Management, as well as a range of other S/NVQs.

D1.1 Gather required information
D1.2 Inform and advise others.

It will also help you develop the following Personal Competences:

- communicating;
- searching for information.

4 Workbook objectives

4.1 The 'Information Age'

There's nothing new about using information to get things done – even cave dwellers needed information, such as how to get to the nearest source of pure water, just to stay alive.

But you will often hear that we now live in the **'Information Age'**. That suggests that information is more important than ever before – perhaps **the** most important thing in modern life.

At one time organizations could be successful simply by investing in physical resources – bigger better factories, nearer to customers, than their competitors' factories, say. The problem was producing enough to satisfy demand.

As competition has increased and become more global there is no significant difference between, say, a Ford factory in Chicago and a Nissan factory in Wales. The problem now is creating enough demand in the first place.

Companies now compete by knowing more about the markets they serve, more about who the best suppliers are, more about how to do things, and – above all – by having the best new ideas. In other words they compete by **gathering information** and **using it intelligently**.

You might not agree that information is the most important thing in your life, but please be aware from the start that good use of information – and information and communications technology – is a skill that is going to be vitally important in your career.

In Session A we will look at the issues surrounding the validity of information, its nature, uses and sources. Then we'll think about **your own** particular information needs at work. Session B will look in more detail at what **methods** you can use to gather this valuable stuff: should you look it up somewhere, or ask other people, or observe and record real-life information for yourself? Some collection methods are computerized, and if you're using those, the chances are you will be storing the information on a computer. We look at the way in which two storage and analysis programs, databases and spreadsheets work. It's important to think about how you will store and analyse your information because it will probably affect how you collect it. Finally we'll tell you about situations when your ability to gather information may be **restricted**, usually by law.

In Session C we'll discuss the great importance of modern **communications technology** in information gathering – most obviously the **Internet**.

4.2 Objectives

At the end of this workbook you should be better able to:

- understand the need for information and gather information relevant to your own area of responsibility;

- identify a range of information sources which may be used in the organization;
- identify means of collecting and recording data and/or information;
- recognize any constraints on the collection of, and access to, data;
- check sources and validity of data;
- use the Internet as an information resource.

5 Activity planner

The following Activities need some planning and you may want to look at them now.

- Activity 3, which asks you to analyse the business activities you undertake and the role of information within them
- Activities 9 and 13, where you are required to prepare a guide to information sources used in your department or workteam for the use of a new recruit
- Activity 14, where you consider the use of automatic data validation in your job
- Activity 19, in which you think about your own team management responsibilities and the information you personally need to do this effectively
- Activity 25, which asks you to audit the data collection devices in use in your organization
- Activity 50, requiring you to log onto the Internet and assess the usefulness of various search tools
- Activity 53, where you consider the actual or possible value of an intranet in your organization

Some of the above Activities may provide the basis of possible acceptable evidence for your S/NVQ portfolio. All Portfolio Activities and the Work-based assignment are signposted with this icon.

This icon will always show the elements to which the Activity or Work-based assignment relates.

Session A
Valid information

1 Introduction

Information is one of the **key resources** of every business. Without information, nobody in an organization could take a single action.

- If you need to contact a supplier you need information. You need to know the supplier's telephone number and address and a contact name.
- If you make Product X you need information. You need to know what materials are needed, what processes they have to go through, and in what order.
- If you are waiting for this month's pay packet – well, you'll have to carry on waiting until the payroll department has collected all the information it needs about your rate of pay, how many hours of overtime you've worked, your tax details, any sick days, and so on.

In this session we'll begin by exploring what information is – particularly what **good information** is – and then we'll think about an organization's different **information needs** in different situations. We'll discuss **sources** of information, and how to make sure that the information you collect is **valid** information.

2 Data and information

Facts and figures are called **data**.

Information is processed data.

Here is an example of data:

The word 'data' is plural, strictly speaking, although most people use it as a singular, at least in ordinary speech.

| A60136/28 | 1,220 | R | 16/06/2003 |
| G22359 | 29,300 | B | 13/07/2003 |

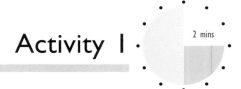

Activity 1   2 mins

What do these numbers and letters tell you?

_____

_____

_____

The best we can say about this example of data is that on 16 June 2003 something happened involving 1,220 of something, and that on 13 July something happened involving 29,300 of something.

What these things are, what happened, how and why, are complete mysteries. They could be stock records, output figures, bank accounts, transaction counts or sales records.

Items of data do not usually convey any meaning on their own. Here is another example.

93   355   213   684   376

Even if you happened to know what these numbers are they don't tell you anything on their own. They are in fact International dialling codes, but they could just as well be pressure readings or the number of customers entering a supermarket over a five-hour period.

Information is data that has been analysed or processed in some way so as to become meaningful.

Country Name	Country Code
Afghanistan	93
Albania	355
Algeria	213
American Samoa	684
Andorra	376

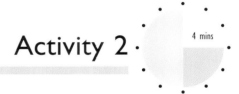

Activity 2

4 mins

Wendy ran her own kitchenware shop. Although she had a wide and varied stock she was often unable to supply what customers wanted. 'Sorry,' she would say 'we had some but they've sold out. I'll have to order some more.' Wendy had plenty of data – invoices and delivery notes from suppliers listing everything she bought in, and her own sales slips listing what she had sold. However she only used these data to work out her monthly accounts and VAT.

What other uses could Wendy make of her sales and purchases data, if she organized them differently?

There is a broad hint in the case study. Wendy does not know the answers to questions such as 'What have I got in stock?' and 'When should I reorder?' The items of data she has could be used to tell her this, provided they are organized and analysed.

■ Providing she knows the true opening stock for each period, she can use sales data to tell her how many of each item she should try to keep in stock. She can then work out when, and how many, she ought to re-order.
■ Wendy could also use the same data to keep track of the value of her stock. This is important for calculating profits, assessing how much insurance she needs, and controlling cash flow.
■ Wendy can use the sales data to show which items sell best and which are most profitable. She can also see how sales vary in the course of the year, and use this to plan for the future (for example, if she closes for an annual holiday it would pay her to do so during a quiet period).

So some quite simple data can reveal some very useful information that will help Wendy make her business more efficient and more profitable. However, 'raw' data does not answer our questions on its own. It has to be processed – in other words, organized and analysed – before it reveals useful information.

The down-side for someone like Wendy, of course, is that it means extra work. If Wendy has to spend several hours more each week writing down lists of figures and doing complicated sums, she may prefer to stay inefficient but relaxed.

It has probably already occurred to you that a computer would help.

■ An electronic till can deal with the sales data automatically.
■ It can link into a computerized accounting system and automatically update it.
■ The accounting system can generate lists, stock reports, sales analyses, orders and other information very quickly.

The system will automatically do her monthly accounts and VAT.

If Wendy makes the move to computerization, she can increase efficiency without having to work any harder – an excellent definition of 'increasing productivity'!

Wendy is of course a very small-scale user of data. Many organizations deal with data on a colossal scale. Imagine the number of individual transactions that have to be dealt with by an organization such as a national chain of supermarkets or a bank with lots of high street branches. There are literally thousands of transactions every minute and computerization is the only way such organizations can record all the data and turn it into useable information.

3 The need for information

3.1 The cycle of business activity

Any business activity – in fact anything you do – can be seen as a cycle, as follows. You may not always consciously work through this cycle for routine activities like making a cup of tea, but it always applies.

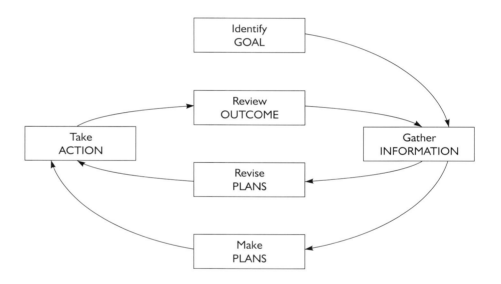

Here's an example to show how this cycle works.

Despina works in the public relations department of a large company.

■   One day she needed to let her company's customers know about recall arrangements for a potentially dangerous product [**Identify GOAL**].
■   She asked the production department to send her full details of the fault. She also checked the feasibility of mailing customers direct, and telephoned various newspapers to find out the cost of placing advertisements [**Gather INFORMATION**].
■   After discussing her findings with the operations director she decided not only to mail distributors of the product but also to advertise the recall in the trade press [**Make PLANS**].
■   She drafted a letter, an advertisement and a press release, and made the appropriate arrangements [**Take ACTION**].

■ A few days after this had been done, Despina asked a member of her staff to ring some of the distributors to check whether they had acted on the letter [**Review OUTCOME**].

■ Discovering that a few claimed not to have received the letter and that some others had not yet withdrawn the faulty product [**Gather more INFORMATION**], she arranged for a telephone follow-up to make doubly sure [**Revise PLANS and Take ACTION**].

Activity 3

10 mins

S/NVQ D1.1

This Activity may provide the basis of appropriate evidence for your S/NVQ portfolio. If you are intending to take this course of action it might be better to write your answers on separate sheets of paper.

Try to analyse two of the main work activities that you undertake in terms of the cycle described above. Concentrate especially on the role of information in your activities.

_____

_____

_____

_____

_____

3.2 Information needs

So, information is an integral part of the cycle of business activity. Organizations need information for a large variety of purposes, but we can identify three broad categories: transactions information; planning and decision-making information; and controlling and performance measurement information.

Recording transactions

There is often a **legal requirement** to record transactions, for example for accounting, tax and audit purposes, or to comply with a contract.

Information about previous transactions can also be used as the raw material for planning and decision-making, and information about current transactions is the raw material for control and performance measurement.

Activity 4 ·

4 mins

Transactions vary widely between organizations. In a newsagent's the sale of a newspaper is a single 'transaction' that at most involves recording data about cash in the till and remaining stock of newspapers. In an insurance company a single transaction might be the issue of an insurance policy involving a large amount of data collection about the customer, the items insured, previous claims history, and so on.

What constitutes a single transaction in your organization and what information has to be recorded?

_____

_____

_____

_____

_____

In most modern businesses collecting transactions data does not involve a great deal of work because it is done by computer programs that automatically capture the data.

As a simple example, if you save a word-processing document the program automatically records information such as the date and time, the number of modifications, the author name, and so on. If you use an accounting package to create a new invoice the program automatically gives it the next invoice number in sequence and won't allow you to override or delete that number.

Planning and decision-making

Once a goal has been identified, the business needs to plan how to achieve it. There will almost always be a variety of ways of getting something done, each of which will have a slightly different outcome.

A decision is a choice of one of a number of possible courses of action. Information is required for any sort of decision: how much the various options will cost, how long each one will take, how many people and machines will be needed, who the best suppliers for materials are, and so on.

Another workbook in this series, *Information in Management*, covers the analysis and use of information to make decisions, in much more detail.

Part of the information for planning and decision-making will be taken from transactions data and part will be taken from the business environment: what customers want, what competitors are doing, what new technologies are available, and so on.

Controlling and performance measurement

Once a plan is put into action, its actual performance must be controlled. Information is needed to assess whether it is going as planned or whether there is some glitch. If there is, it may be necessary to take some form of corrective action.

Again, the information required will be partly taken from transactions data and partly from the business environment.

4 Good information

To be truly useful information needs to possess certain qualities, so let's think about the factors that are important for the successful conversion of data to information. These can be summed up in a useful mnemonic: ACCURATE.

A	Accurate
C	Complete
C	Clear
U	User-targeted
R	Relevant
A	Authoritative
T	Timely
E	Economic

To be truly useful information needs to possess **all** of these qualities **in the right measure**. Many of the qualities are closely **linked**. For instance, the completeness of information will depend on what the user will use the information for. The ideal timeliness of information depends, among other things, on how economic it is to produce the information in that timescale.

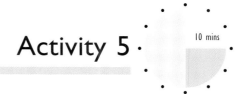

Activity 5

10 mins

Before you read on see if you can write a few words about each of the eight qualities in the ACCURATE mnemonic, explaining why **you** think each one makes information more useful.

_____

_____

_____

_____

_____

_____

_____

Accurate

Information should be as accurate as the user needs it to be.

Sometimes that means absolute precision, for instance if you are telling someone what telephone number they should ring.

Sometimes absolute precision is not possible. For instance, if you witness a car accident it is obviously better if you can tell the police the precise make and model of the car involved, but if all you can remember is that 'it was a big dark-coloured car', that still helps the police quite a lot.

However, information should only be **accurate enough for its purpose** and there is no need to go into unnecessary detail – just because you can – for pointless accuracy.

You and your workteam are likely to need information that is accurate to the nearest penny, minute or kilogram. For example, purchase department staff have to pay suppliers exactly what they are owed. If a task cannot be done in less than 18 minutes it is unreasonable to say 'it takes about a quarter of an hour' and expect your team to do four an hour.

Your own manager might be content with figures rounded to the nearest 100 or 1,000 since greater detail would serve no purpose. For example, in budgeting sales figures are often rounded to the nearest £1,000 because the figures are only a guess and the actual figures will be affected by things that can't be controlled, such as how many customers decide to buy your organization's products.

Very senior managers might only need figures to the nearest 10,000, or even 100,000 or million. At this level of decision-making very precise estimates are not relevant: the odd hundred will make no difference to the overall decision. If you find this hard to understand, imagine you want to buy, say, a new computer and you have £200 to spend. You would not care whether a new computer costs £563 or £597.50, because you couldn't afford one anyway! It would be enough to tell you that a new computer costs 'about three times more' than you have available to spend.

Complete

This does not mean that you have to have every known fact about a subject, but that you should have all the information you need to make the right decision.

- **Nothing important should be left out.** For example, a credit controller who notices that a customer owes £20,000 and that the debt is now four months old might decide to write a strongly-worded letter to the customer, demanding immediate payment. Now suppose that, without the credit controller's knowledge, the customer had been offered special credit terms of six months. Sending a strongly-worded demand for payment would be a mistake likely to create bad feeling and damage the prospects of future sales to the customer.
- **Nothing *unimportant* should be left in.** There are limits to how much people can absorb and understand properly. If there is too much detail the reader suffers **information overload**. In the above example, the credit controller does not need to know the name, address and account number of every other customer with six-month credit terms, just that some customers are allowed longer to pay than others. So this is something to check before sending the boys round!

Clear

Information must be clear to people who use it. If they don't understand it properly they won't be able to use it properly. It is therefore important to choose the right channel of communication and the most appropriate way of presenting it.

Some information is best communicated by telephone or in a face-to-face meeting, whereas other information can only be communicated effectively in writing and figures.

Presentation can have a major impact on the value of information. A business report, for example, is far more likely to be read in full and acted upon if it begins with a clear title, a contents page and a succinct summary, and ends with an index and explanation of any technical terms. It is far more likely to be understood if the detailed part has clearly tabulated facts and figures and lots of visual summaries, such as pie charts and bar charts.

Activity 6 · 5 mins

Here are the rules for the format of UK postcodes.

The total length must be six, seven, or eight characters, and a single space
  character must be included in the third, fourth or fifth position.
The first part of the code, to the left of the space, can be two, three, or four
  characters.
The first character of the first part of the code must be a letter.
The second part, to the right of the space, must always be three characters.
The first character of the second part must be a (one-digit) number.
The second and third characters of the second part must be letters.
The letters I and Z are not used in position two.
The second half of the code never uses the letters C, I, K, M, O, and V.
The sole exception is the Girobank postcode (GIR 0AA).

See if you can find a simpler, **clearer** way of presenting this information.

_____

_____

_____

_____

A suggested answer to this activity can be found on page 122.

User-targeted

Good information is tailored to the needs of the people who will use it. For instance, if the information will only ever be used by you and your team members you can feel free to use any in-house jargon that is commonly understood within your part of the organization, such as an abbreviated name for a product, like C04X. If, on the other hand, you were telling a customer about the same product you should use the full name.

We've looked at other examples of user-targeted information already under the headings 'accuracy' and 'completeness': information should be just as accurate and complete as the user needs it to be.

Activity 7 · 4 mins

Who are the users of an organization's information who should be borne in mind when considering whether it is properly user-targeted?

_____

_____

_____

_____

Internal users of information include the board of the company (or the equivalent of a board in other organizations); divisional managers; departmental heads; first line managers such as you; and your team members (some of whom may work on their own initiative while others work to your precise instructions).

Information flows up and down between these levels and it also flows horizontally, for instance between you and other first line managers or between individual members of your team.

Some information is relevant to people **outside your organization** as well as to its managers and employees. For example:

- an organization's **suppliers** and **customers** use information to decide whether or not to trade with the organization;
- the organization's **bankers** take decisions affecting the amount of money they are prepared to lend;
- the **Inland Revenue** and **HM Customs and Excise** authorities require information for taxation and VAT purposes;
- other **government** departments (for example the Department of Trade and Industry) regularly require organizational information;
- the **public** might have an interest in information relating to an organization's products or services;
- the **media** (newspapers, television, etc.) use information generated by organizations in news stories.

Relevant

Information must be relevant to the purpose for which the user wants to use it. Sometimes this is obvious. For instance if you ask what the weather is like and someone tells you 'it is 3.30 pm' you have not collected any relevant information to help answer your question. Likewise, if someone else tells you 'it was sunny yesterday', that is totally irrelevant.

Usually, however, the relevance of a piece of information depends on the circumstances.

■ If you want an estimate of sales in August then it will often be relevant to look at the figure for July's sales and at the figure for sales in August last year. But sometimes – for instance if you are going to launch an entirely new range of products this August – historic data is of little or no relevance.

■ Suppose you were preparing a report about the launch of a new product in a new market and you included the information that the currency in the United Arab Emirates is called the 'dirham'. That might be relevant if you were reporting to your manager in England. But if you were writing the report for people who live in the United Arab Emirates it would be common knowledge and not worth including.

■ Sometimes, as we've seen, figures to the nearest penny are relevant. But to some users the pennies may be irrelevant.

Authoritative

By this we mean that the **source** of the information should be as reliable as possible. Information that you read in the **Financial Times** or hear on the **BBC** is authoritative because those organizations employ a large number of experts and risk being sued if they get things wrong. Information that you overhear in the pub is not authoritative (although it may be correct).

Authoritativeness is an increasingly important concern because so much information is now available and accessible from such a large number of sources.

It is also an issue when considering internally-produced information. Managers are less likely to trust information from their staff if they know that a report was prepared by inexperienced members of the team who do not yet have a full understanding of the area they work in and the use to which their information will be put.

We'll discuss the authoritativeness of information in more detail later in this session when we talk about information sources and the validity of information.

Timely

Information needs to be available **at the time when** a decision is made.

For example, suppose a company expects a new product to be available from 3 June and intends to book the advertising space on 5 May. If there is any doubt about meeting the 3 June deadline then that information needs to be available **on 5 May**.

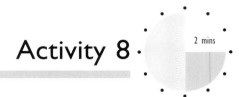

Activity 8 · 2 mins

A colleague tells you that information should always be prepared early and it should be prepared as regularly as possible. Do you agree?

Timely does **not** necessarily mean **early**. If your train leaves early there is a good chance you will miss it. Likewise if you provide managers with information before they are ready to deal with it, it may be overlooked.

Information prepared **too frequently** can be a serious disadvantage, too. If, for example, a decision is regularly taken at a monthly meeting, information to make the decision is only required once a month. Preparing weekly reports would be a time-consuming waste of effort.

Economic

The **benefits** obtained from information must be **greater than** the **costs** of collecting and analysing it.

This is mainly a matter of **how long** it takes to prepare the information and **what resources** are needed. For example, it might be interesting and useful to get every member of your team to write down everything they do, every minute of the day, and then prepare a complex summary at the erd of the week. However, if they all spend their time doing this it is unlikely that they will get much real work done. And if you spend the time needed to analyse the data they give you then you won't get much real work done either!

If the information is really worth having it is worth looking into more efficient methods of collecting and analysing the underlying data. That is one of the main topics in Session B of this book.

5 Information sources

5.1 Internal sources

Organizations **create** large amounts of information in the course of their daily work.

EXTENSION 1
For more about management research see this helpful guide by Mark Easterby-Smith and Richard Thorpe

■ A great deal of information is **sent out** to others, such as letters, invoices and statements sent to customers, brochures, price lists and promotional material, orders for materials, cheques or BACS payments sent to suppliers.
■ A great deal of formal information **flows around** the organization: e-mails, memos, notices on notice boards, minutes of meetings, internal reports such as performance reports or information about the future such as business plans.
■ There is also information required to **operate internal systems**, especially the **accounting system**, but also supporting records such as job cards, timesheets, clocking-in systems and stock requisitions. Such documents record time spent and materials or other resources used in making an item or doing a task.
■ In most organizations there are also all sorts of **rule books**, operational manuals, technical drawings, procedural guidelines, lists of approved suppliers, policy documents, and reports on incidents, disputes and other issues that have arisen in the past.
■ There are often numerous other paper records in organizations. **Administrative records** are often kept for long periods because they may have a legal significance one day. These include:
■ records of disciplinary and appraisal interviews;
■ records of health and safety audits, environmental health inspections, and so on;
■ staff training records;
■ records relating to staff recruitment.

Finally it is important not to forget that there will be an enormous amount of **informal communication** and information exchange between managers and their workteams and between individual members of workteams, whether this is across the desk, by the coffee machine, over the telephone, in the pub after work or by some other means.

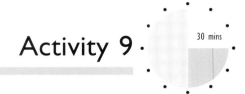

Activity 9   30 mins

S/NVQ D1.1,
D1.2

This Activity may provide the basis of appropriate evidence for your S/NVQ portfolio. If you are intending to take this course of action it might be better to write your answers on separate sheets of paper.

Prepare a guide to the internal information sources used by your workteam suitable for use by a new recruit.

(You may prefer to do this Activity at the same time as Activity 13 which asks you to prepare a similar guide listing your workteam's main external information sources.)

5.2 External sources

Organizations also collect large amounts of information from external sources – invoices, letters, advertisements, tax demands and so on **received from** customers and suppliers and various authorities.

Informal gathering of information from outside sources also goes on all the time, consciously or unconsciously, because the employees of an organization take an interest in the world around them – they read newspapers, watch television, have experiences outside work and talk to other people in other jobs.

However, there are many occasions when an active search outside the organization is necessary. So where do you look?

Primary and secondary information sources

A **primary source** of information is as close as you can get to the origin of an item of information: an eyewitness report, the original document (for instance a birth certificate), and so on.

A **secondary source** provides 'second hand' information: books, articles, verbal or written reports by someone else. There are a huge number of secondary sources, if you know what you want, and where to look for it.

If it is essential to get information from the primary source you will need to interview people, make your own observations and do original research. This requires time and probably money. You need will to identify the right people to talk to, the right documents to see, and so on. When you find them you will need to ask the right questions and record the right details, so that you end up with the answers you needed.

Sometimes you will have no option but to seek out the primary source, particularly if:

- it is a sensitive personal matter, in which case it should be discussed directly with the person concerned;
- you suspect that secondary sources can't be relied on;
- the topic is so important that extra time and money can be justified.

Session B covers methods of obtaining **primary** information.

We'll be talking about **secondary sources** for the rest of this session.

5.3 Secondary sources

The **Internet** is of course the richest secondary source of information of all – on practically any subject you can think of (and many that you can't think of!). Not all of it is good information, however. And although in theory it is easy to search the Internet, in practice it often takes longer to find exactly what you want than another method would have taken.

Because it is so important, the Internet is discussed in much more detail in **Session C**.

Here we'll concentrate on more traditional sources.

Radio and television stations

Most of us get our general knowledge about what is happening in the world from radio and TV: either general news programmes, or documentaries on specific topics, or consumer-related regulars like holiday or fashion programmes.

There are a number of programmes dedicated specifically to business issues, especially on **news-only** channels like Sky News or BBC News 24. Cable and satellite provide other specialist channels on various topics and the number will continue to grow.

There are also local radio stations which often provide information about local services and activities, gathered from local organizations.

Ceefax and **Teletext** are television-based services provided by the BBC, ITV and the various satellite and cable TV companies. Information offered includes national and local news, weather and travel reports, stock market and personal finance information, and general interest topics such as sports results, recipes, cinema listings, and so on.

Newspapers

Newspapers are the source of information that most of us use to find out more about things that we heard on TV or radio yesterday. Tabloids such as the *Sun* and the *Mirror* confine themselves mainly to lifestyle issues, celebrities and sport. The *Mail* and the *Express* do likewise but they also have more in-depth coverage of business and political issues and more foreign news.

For business information the richest sources are the broadsheet newspapers such as *The Financial Times, The Times, The Telegraph, The Guardian, The Independent, the Glasgow Herald,* and *Western Mail.*

Activity 10 · Ongoing

Try and get into the habit of reading the business sections of a broadsheet newspaper at least twice a week if you do not already do so. It does not matter which one you choose: your preference will be partly determined by your political views and other interests. A good way to start is to visit your local library and look through the 'serious' newspapers there.

Persevere with this activity: you will gradually get used to the language used and the topics covered.

Magazines

EXTENSION 2
A range of magazines is available in this area

Most business categories are served by several weekly or monthly 'trade' journals, and magazines such as *The Grocer* for the food and drink industry or *Computing* for people who work in the IT industry. Your organization probably subscribes to the magazines and journals that are relevant to what it does.

Consumer magazines like *Which?* and *What PC?* may also be useful sources of business information if your organization produces consumer goods or needs to buy such things.

Specialist providers of information

A number of organizations provide specialist information, including:

- **advice or information bureaux**. These provide information in their own particular field in the form of one-to-one advice, information leaflets and fact sheets. Examples include Citizens Advice Bureaux; Offices of Fair Trading; Tourist Information offices, and so on. **Commercial high street organizations** like travel agents and estate agents may also be helpful up to a point (but only because they want to sell you something!).
- **news and information agencies** such as Reuters or LexisNexis. These organizations collect information from reporters and eye witnesses of events and from a vast range of publications, then organize and analyse it and sell it to newspapers, governments, companies and academics, usually on a **subscription** basis.
- **consultancies** and **research organizations** of all sorts. Some of these concentrate on a specific aspect of business (telecoms or warehouse technology, say) while others have more general expertise (for example MORI). They produce reports for general sale, and also accept commissions to do primary research for individual organizations.
- **subscription-based organizations**. The Institute of Directors, the Confederation of British Industry and the Federation of Small Businesses are just some good sources of general business information for those who subscribe to them.
- **professional bodies** such as the Law Society, the Institute of Chartered Accountants in England and Wales, or the Direct Marketing Association offer a certain amount of information about their specialist topic to the general public and a good deal more to their members. In particular they produce **best practice standards**, which their members are expected to follow.
- the **British Standards Institution** (BSI). This produces a huge range of detailed specifications for every imaginable product.

Libraries

Some libraries are part of the **public library** system; others are associated with a **college** or a **professional body**, in which case access may be limited to members or suitably qualified people, or subject to other access criteria.

If you are only familiar with a small local public library that stocks mainly fiction it is worth getting to know where the **main** reference library in your area is and paying a visit. Such libraries generally have large collections of newspapers and journals going back several years: all you have to do is ask at the counter. There will also be a wide range of **reference books**. We'll discuss these in a moment.

Your organization may well have **its own library**. Sometimes in a small organization a non-specialist member of staff looks after it. Larger organizations often have extensive libraries with full-time library staff.

There are various approaches to finding useful information in a library, whether you know the author and title of a particular book or article or not. Most have computerized catalogues. That may be all you need, but if you can't find something don't be afraid to ask. The library staff will point you in the right direction: that's their job!

Activity 11

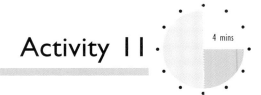

4 mins

Books and articles often contain references to **other** books and articles in footnotes or in lists of references at the end. These are usually in a format designed to help you find the original book or article itself. Here are three samples. Your task is to explain what these references mean.

Torrington D, Hall, L, Taylor, S, *Human Resource Management*, FT Prent ce Hall, 2001 (ISBN: 0273646397), pp 34–36.

Pascale, R, Athod, A, & Goss, T, 'The reinvention rollercoaster', *Harvard Business Review*, November–December, 1993, pp 25–26.

Curtis, J, 'Cutting the cost of Internet calls', *Marketing*, 8 July 1999, pp 25–6.

_____

_____

_____

_____

_____

The first example is a reference to a book. Books are normally quoted something like this:

■ Author (surname, initials), *title (in italics)*, publisher (and sometimes the place of publication), date of publication, pages referred to ('p' = page, 'pp' = pages).

Sometimes you are given the ISBN, which stands for International Standard Book Number. This is used by booksellers and publishers to uniquely identify any book. If you know a book's ISBN you can often use it as a quick way of searching a library catalogue by computer.

The second example is a reference to an article in a fairly learned periodical published bi-monthly, while the third is a reference to an article in *Marketing* magazine, published weekly. Articles in a periodical, magazine or newspaper are quoted as follows:

Author (surname, initials), 'title of article', *title of periodical (italics)*, possibly the volume and number, date, pages referred to.

Note that you are always told the **date** of publication. This can be very useful if it is important to collect recent information or information that takes account of, say, legislation up to a certain date.

5.4 Reference books

Reference books are a rich secondary source of any item of information you might want to find. If you keep two or three good reference books near your desk plus a loose-leaf file of your own often-used information, you can save yourself hours on the Internet!

But knowing the right book to use, and using it well, is a skill in itself.

- **Dictionaries**. Make sure you always have access to a good dictionary of the English language, and don't be embarrassed to use it if you are in doubt about the spelling or the meaning of a word (or its pronunciation if you have to use it in conversation). There are also dictionaries or glossaries covering specific subjects. If you deal regularly with solicitors, have a dictionary of legal terms available; if you deal with engineers or bio-technicians a dictionary of science is handy.

- A **thesaurus** can be very useful when you need to find the right word or phrase for a particular situation . . . but only if you know the precise meaning you are looking for to start with! Roget's Thesaurus is the best known. This lists words and phrases categorized by topic and sub-topic (for instance 'Intellect: Creative Thought'). Have a browse through one, starting with the index at the back.

- There are also various **writing guides**: guides to English grammar, guides to punctuation, guides to business letter-writing, titles and forms of address, pronunciation of names, and so on. Any of these might help when dealing with specific problems.

- **Almanacs** are general sources of factual information, published annually. For example **Whitaker's Almanac** is useful for: central, regional and local government, countries, education, environmental issues, finance, health, heritage, information technology, institutions and charities, law, media, Parliament, political and economic facts and statistics, religion, royalty, societies, sport, taxation, and transport. (Pretty useful to have next time you do a pub quiz!) There is an index at the back to help you find information quickly, and you should make sure you are using an **up-to-date** edition.

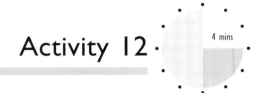

Activity 12

Many people just jump into reference books without taking the trouble to find out how they 'work', and then get frustrated that they cannot find the information they are looking for.

Look at a reference book such as a dictionary or an almanac and take the time to learn the best way of using it. Somewhere in the front pages there will be some kind of guide to 'how to use this book', and there may be a variety of other information in the front and back pages. Read that information!

Note down the reference book you studied here (not forgetting what you learned earlier about references to books).

- **Atlases** and **road maps** often contain more than just maps. They may also give information on population distribution, social trends, major industries and politics. As usual you should check the date of publication of any atlas or road map you consult, as they go out of date quickly.
- **Timetables** and **itineraries** such as rail guides, air travel guides and various timetables will be important sources of information if you or your team need to make travel arrangements. Timetables often use symbols to get as much information on the page as possible: these will be explained in a 'key' somewhere on each page or in an introduction.
- The **Phone Book** and **Yellow Pages** or **Business Pages** are useful sources of information. It is well worth getting to know your way about the **introductory pages** of your phone books. For instance the introduction to the SW London Yellow Pages gives information about local emergency numbers, council services, environmental services, transport, trading standards, citizen's advice, local amenities and street maps.
- There may well be **specific reference works** associated with your line of work. If you work in the drinks trade you might have the **Oxford Companion to Wine** by your side. In a tax department of a firm of accountants you would use well-respected tax guides like **Tolley's** or other **Butterworth's** publications. If you work for a car dealer your 'bible' might be **Glass's Guide** which lists recommended second-hand values for vehicles.

5.5 Government

Central and local **government bodies** are perhaps the largest providers of information of all. They produce all sorts of guidelines, leaflets, reports, statistics, and so on.

Selection of government and public service organization information sources

Advertising Standards Authority	Independent regulatory body for non-broadcast advertisements in the UK
Bank of England	The central bank for the United Kingdom
British Library	The national library of the United Kingdom
Business Link	Advice and information for new and small businesses
Census 2001	Information on the 2001 Census and links to previous censuses
Central Office of Information	The government's communications division
Commission for Racial Equality	Tackles racial discrimination and promotes racial equality
Companies House	Company registry and information resource
Competition Commission	Monitors business competition and ensures fair trading
Customs and Excise, Her Majesty's	Collects duties and taxes and controls imports and exports.
Department for Education and Skills	Responsible for education and work-based learning
Department for Environment, Food and Rural Affairs	Responsible for the environment, food and rural affairs
Department for Transport	Central government department responsible for transport
Department for Work and Pensions	Responsible for jobs and benefits
Department of Health	Responsible for all aspects of health
Department of Trade and Industry	Responsible for economic development and UK competitiveness
Employment Appeal Tribunal	Handles appeals arising from employment disputes
Equal Opportunities Commission	Works to remove sex discrimination in Britain
Financial Services Authority	Regulates financial services in the UK
General Register Office	Ensures all births, marriages and deaths are registered and maintains a central archive
Health and Safety Executive	Regulates health and safety in the workplace
Her Majesty's Stationery Office	Manages and regulates government information
Home Office	Responsible for internal affairs in England and Wales
Information Commissioner	Responsible for the Data Protection and Freedom of Information Acts
Inland Revenue	Responsible for the administration of taxes
Investors in People UK	Encourages organizations to invest in their staff
National Weights and Measures Laboratory	Ensures UK measurements are accurate, fair and legal
Office for National Statistics	Collects and distributes official UK statistics
Office of Fair Trading	Protection for UK consumers
Office of Telecommunications (OFTEL)	Regulates the telecommunications industry
Patent Office	Responsible for intellectual property rights in the UK
Public Record Office (PRO)	The official archive of UK government and law records
Queen's Awards for Industry	UK awards for business performance
Skills and Labour Market Information	Provides information on the labour market in the UK
Small Business Service	Government agency providing information, advice and assistance for small businesses
Trading Standards	Information on trading standards and consumer protection
Treasury	Responsible for the UK economy and public finances
United Kingdom Accreditation Service	Accredits laboratories and certification and inspection bodies
Vehicle Inspectorate	Ensures that motor vehicles are maintained to minimum legal standards.

Source: extracted from http://www.ukonline.gov.uk/ © Crown copyright

Above is a list of **just a few** of the many central government departments and organizations in the UK that may be useful sources of business information. This is just to give you an idea of the vast wealth of information available: you can find a list of over 1,000 government and public service organizations at http://www.ukonline.gov.uk/.

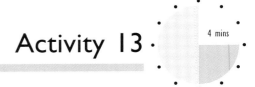

Activity 13

4 mins

On separate sheets of paper prepare a guide to the **external** information sources used by your workteam, suitable for use by a new recruit.

(You may prefer to do this Activity at the same time as Activity 9 which asks you to prepare a similar guide listing your workteam's main internal information sources.)

6 Checking validity

Information that you collect should be good information, in all its many senses.

If you like, valid information is information that possesses the two As of good information: Accuracy and Authority.

There are two main reasons why information may not be valid:

- if it was **not recorded correctly**, for instance if you wrote down 369 instead of 396;
- if it was incorrect in the first place because you used an **unreliable source**.

6.1 Checking data entry

The most obvious way of making sure that you have recorded a piece of information correctly is to **double check** once you have written it down or typed it in. You probably do this sub-consciously all the time, for instance when you write a cheque. You may well do it when you are taking down details over the phone, by reading back what you have written to the person you are speaking to.

The trouble with double-checking, of course, is that it takes at least twice as long!

Fortunately, most data is recorded by computer these days, and computers can help by checking the validity of data as it is input and alerting the user and refusing to accept the data if it is incorrect.

There are limits to this, because a computer can only detect certain types of errors but it is still immensely useful. The main types of computer validation checks are as follows.

Format checks

These ensure that the data entered is in an appropriate format, for example if a number is expected the computer will check that the data entered does not contain letters or punctuation marks other than the decimal point. A postcode is a more elaborate example: the computer will test the data entered to make sure it conforms to the pattern of letters and numbers that we outlined earlier in this session.

Range checks

These try to make sure that the data lies within predetermined limits. For instance, if we had asked you to write down a number between 390 and 400 and you wrote down 369 or 425 your data would be rejected.

This has a number of business applications. If you were recording purchases, for instance, the computer may be able to match the prices you enter with a database of suppliers' price lists, and then print out a list of prices which differed from the database price by plus or minus 10%, say. (Some allowance would have to be made because suppliers change their prices or allow discounts.) You would then only have to double check the exceptions, not every single entry.

Limit checks

Limit checks are similar to range checks. They check that data is not above or below a **specific** value.

For example, a computerized timesheet may prevent your team member from entering a value for hours worked in one day of more than 24 or less than 0.

Existence checks

These checks make sure that you do not enter data about things that don't exist. For example if you are recording a customer's order and you accidentally type in a stock code that is not used, the system will alert you to this and will not allow you to continue until you correct the error.

Of course, if you type in a stock code that does exist but is not the item the customer ordered the computer will know nothing about it. To help avoid this you will often find that computer systems will prompt you with more information once you have entered a code number. For example if you type in the code 400/4253 the computer might automatically display the description 'combination microwave oven'. If you knew that the customer had ordered a hairdryer there is a good chance that you would notice the discrepancy!

Calculation checks

The computer may have pre-programmed rules for various types of calculation. For instance if an invoice has a net value of £100 and VAT is set at 17.5%, the computer will make sure that the figure entered for VAT is £17.50.

Activity 14

S/NVQ D1.1

This Activity may provide the basis of appropriate evidence for your S/NVQ portfolio. If you are intending to take this course of action it might be better to write your answers on separate sheets of paper.

It may not have occurred to you before that the systems you use at work include all sorts of automatic checks to validate data entry.

■ Make a note of any automatic checks used in your work
■ Consider whether any new automatic checks could be introduced
■ Where work has to be validated in another way explain why an automatic check would not be suitable or feasible

6.2 Checking the source

Checking whether the source of your information is reliable is once again a matter of double-checking – except that this time you check against a **different** source.

Checking against what you know for certain

Quite often the second source is **information or experience that you possess**. For example:

- if someone tells you that England won the football World Cup in 2002 and you happen to know that this is quite untrue – perhaps because you witnessed England lose to Brazil in the quarter finals, live on television, and were very upset about it – you would dismiss the information as invalid;
- you might read a political pamphlet that tells you that public transport has 'improved by 30%' in the last six months. But if you have just had your longest ever journey home, because of delays on local trains and buses, you would dismiss the information as invalid – or at least, misleading, even if the average percentage figure happens to be correct.

Checking against what you think is reasonable

Often, even though you may not know the precise facts, you will have an idea whether a piece of information is likely to be reasonable. For instance, if you read in a newspaper article that 'the basic rate of income tax in Country X is 90%' you would probably want to check that this information is correct because you know that the basic rate of income tax in your own country is much lower than 90%.

How well you can do this depends partly on the subject matter and partly on general knowledge.

Checking against what you can easily find out

For example, suppose you receive an invoice from an outside supplier. You should easily be able to check it against the order that **you** placed with the supplier – in other words with a document or documents generated by someone in **your** organization. This is just a matter of knowing your organization's system.

Activity 15

3 mins

What danger or dangers can you see in these three types of checking?

_____

_____

_____

The answer to this activity can be found on page 122.

Checking by conducting further research

Let's go back to the example of the information that 'the basic rate of income tax in Country X is 90%'. Your first thought should be that the rate seems rather high and the information may not be valid.

In this case the best course of action is to find a second external source of the same information, independent from the first source and preferably more authoritative. The obvious place to look in this case would be the website of the tax authorities in the country in question, which should be authoritative. If there is no website it ought to be possible to find a telephone number. Failing that, you could contact a firm of tax consultants or accountants, ideally one with an office in the country concerned.

The general principles here are simple:

■ ask yourself who is the original source of the information and, if possible, consult their version of the information;
■ failing that, ask yourself who is likely to have the strongest interest in getting the information correct and consult their version of the information.

6.3 Evaluating opinions

The ideal, of course, is that you only ever collect information from sources that are 100% reliable: publications or people that always provide good, ACCURATE information. But this won't always be possible in real life.

Let's look at a mini scenario to see what problems might arise in practice.

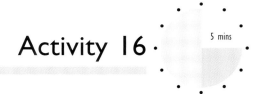

Activity 16

5 mins

Tom's team was soon to be amalgamated with another smaller team to form a single sales department for the educational market. Tom's boss, Janine, asked him to brief her on how work would be organized and how his own role as first line manager would be affected.

Tom's precise words were as follows:

'I don't see any problem. We're taking on an extra range of products, but the people who are joining us presumably have the right level of product knowledge and I imagine their sales culture and paperwork are much the same as ours. How many are coming, did you say? Six. Right, well obviously that will mean more work for me, but I'm confident that I can cope. Basically, it'll just be matter of deciding who handles what accounts. Oh, and there may be some sorting out to do on the sales databases. They probably have their own. Anyway I'm looking forward to the challenge! When do we start by the way?'

Tom seems confident, but should Janine be? Explain your answer.

_____

_____

_____

_____

_____

_____

_____

Janine has asked Tom for information, and he seems confident. But his response should worry her deeply.

- He hasn't got a grip on the basic facts – such as when the change is to take place and how many people are involved.
- He hasn't briefed himself on the team that is joining his, their work or their procedures.
- He hasn't given much thought to the problems involved in combining two work teams and two different sales databases.
- He hasn't given any thought to how he could use this change as an opportunity to improve work practices and efficiency.

In other words, there's a lot of opinion here, but very few facts and figures. And even the opinions are suspect.

There is a world of difference between the schoolchild who says 'Scotland will beat Morocco easily' and a barrister who says 'your chance of winning this case is around 80%'. The barrister is giving an expert opinion. Experience, training, skill and a careful study of the case law have gone into it, and the opinion is worth taking seriously.

On the other hand, no sane person would mortgage the house and put the money on Scotland winning on the basis of a tip from a ten-year-old.

The barrister may be wrong, and the child may be right, but a serious evaluation suggests that the barrister's opinion can be trusted, whereas the child's cannot.

When you are trying to evaluate an opinion, you can use a simple checklist to assess the reliability and credibility of the source of the information.

Views, feelings and opinions – a reliability checklist		
1	Is the source experienced in this field?	
2	Does the source understand the issues?	
3	Does the source have access to up-to-date information?	
4	Has the source consulted other appropriate sources?	
5	Is the source free of personal biases about the matter?	
6	Does the source have a good track record for giving reliable opinions?	
7	Is the opinion consistent with other information available?	

Instead of just ticking, you could rate the source on a 0–5 scale for each question and add up the totals. A score of more than 25 on these seven questions would indicate a high level of reliability; less than 15 would not inspire confidence.

Activity 17

4 mins

We naturally place more reliance on information when it comes from someone we respect and trust.

What other factors do you think can make views, feelings and opinions seem more reliable than perhaps they are?

_____

_____

_____

_____

If an evaluation of information produced high scores on every item in the checklist above except the last, how would you react?

_____

_____

_____

_____

There are many subtle factors that influence our confidence in the information we receive.

Experience in sales and marketing shows that most people are influenced by:

■ high-quality presentation, with well-designed print and graphics;
■ the confidence with which the information is delivered;
■ the general image of the organization and people from which the information comes;
■ association of the information with trusted public figures (in advertising, etc.).

On the second point in the Activity, if an experienced and trusted opinion doesn't tie up with the other information available, then it would be prudent to re-examine that information before reaching a decision.

Self-assessment 1

10 mins

1 Give three reasons why organizations record transactions information.

_____

_____

_____

2 What do we mean when we say that information should possess the following qualities?

■ Authority

_____

■ Clarity

_____

■ Economy

_____

3 Is 'valid' information the same as 'good' information?

_____

_____

_____

4 What is the difference between a primary source of information and a secondary source?

_____

_____

_____

_____

5   List five types of specialist information provider and give an example of each.

_____

_____

_____

_____

_____

_____

6   Describe three types of computer validation check.

_____

_____

_____

_____

7   What are four ways of double-checking the source of information?

_____

_____

_____

_____

_____

Answers to these questions can be found on pages 118–119.

7 Summary

- Organizations cannot function without information, and moreover this is the 'information age', where organizations compete by having better information and using it more intelligently than others.

- Information is the name given to raw facts and figures (data) once they have been processed (organized and analysed) and become meaningful.

- Information is a key part of the cycle of business activities: simple recording of transactions, planning and decision-making, and control and performance measurement.

- Good information is ACCURATE, that is:
  - Accurate
  - Complete
  - Clear
  - User-targeted
  - Relevant
  - Authoritative
  - Timely
  - Economic

- Internal sources of information include: correspondence sent to suppliers and customers and related accounting information; information related to internal systems such as time sheets; procedures manuals; and administrative records such as training records.

- External sources include information received from customers and suppliers and a vast array of published information: TV, newspapers, magazines, reference books of all kinds, information provided by specialist bodies, government information and, above all, the Internet.

- Information may not be valid either because it is recorded wrongly or because the source is not reliable.

- Various automatic checks can be used to ensure that data is recorded correctly.

- Sources can be checked against what you know for certain or judge to be reasonable, or they can be compared with other internal or external sources.

- Extra care is needed when you are evaluating information that is merely someone's opinion. Are they an expert? Are they biased? Do other sources agree?

Session B
Collecting and recording information

1 Introduction

Today the ability to collect data is almost limitless, thanks to the growth of information and communications technology (ICT). There is a strong temptation to collect more and more of it because the technology has made most kinds of data much easier to collect, and all kinds of data much easier to store.

In this session we are going to begin by considering what sort of information managers typically need to collect to enable them to manage their teams effectively, and we ask you to consider what information is **relevant to your particular job**.

Then we will move on to look at the **means** of collecting data through automatic recording using monitoring devices such as pressure mats or cameras, and computerized input devices such as bar code readers in shops or keypads on cash machines. We'll also mention some of the new data collection technology that is just starting to have an impact.

If you are using electronic or computerized means of collecting information, the chances are you will be storing and analysing it on a computer. Your method of storage and analysis may well affect how you go about collecting information. We move on to an overview of **databases** and **spreadsheets**, two methods of computerized storage and analysis.

In spite of these developments there will often be occasions when the best way of collecting information is to talk to people and ask them **questions**, so the next two parts of this session look in detail at various questioning techniques, and describe how to devise a **questionnaire**, conduct a **survey** or carry out an **observation** exercise.

Finally we will think about the **constraints on collecting data**. In fact there are very few constraints other than obtaining permission and paying a price, but there are legal considerations if you want to **store** the data and **reuse** it. In particular we will discuss the Data Protection Act 1998 and issues relating to copyright.

2 Information relevant to your job

People who run organizations need information that answers questions like:

- have our targets been reached?
- what did it cost to run the organization last year?
- how much money do we owe our suppliers?
- how big an overdraft do we need?
- what proportion of our costs is accounted for by wages, overheads, materials, etc.?

To answer these questions, they need to collect information about every aspect of the organization.

Likewise, the information you need depends on the work that you and your workteam do, what resources you need to do it, and what is expected of you.

Activity 18

Read through the two lists below.

■ Tick Column 1 if this is something for which you have a personal responsibility.

■ Tick Column 2 as well if you need information in order to fulfil this responsibility.

Responsibilities affecting today	1	2	Responsibilities affecting the future	1	2
Allocating work			Planning activities		
Monitoring progress against targets			Developing staff for tomorrow's needs		
Dealing with problems			Spotting/defusing potential problems		
Maintaining productivity			Seeking ways to improve productivity		
Controlling costs					

Most first line managers and team leaders would have ticked all the items in both columns. If there was anything that you didn't tick, you might be advised to rethink because:

■ you may in practice have a responsibility there, even if this isn't stated formally;

■ all these responsibilities involve making decisions, and without information you can only make good decisions by accident.

For instance, imagine a manager who is in charge of the order dispatch department in a garment factory. Here are the manager's main information needs for each of the categories above.

Responsibilities affecting today	What the manager needs to know
Allocating work	Who is available to work What their skills are What orders are to go to what customers, and when
Monitoring progress against targets	When each order has been readied, and when it has been dispatched
Dealing with problems	What the problems are
Maintaining productivity	Productivity targets and performance measures
Controlling costs	Budgets for expenses, overtime etc.; costs of different dispatch methods

Responsibilities affecting the future	What the manager needs to know
Planning future activities	Financial constraints, output forecasts, planned technical developments
Developing staff for tomorrow's needs	What those needs are likely to be
Spotting/defusing potential problems	About the business and about staff
Seeking ways to improve productivity	Productivity data and targets for the future

Some of this information will be formally recorded, especially anything that incurs a significant cost such as salaries, materials and outside services like delivery.

However, there are many items of information in the list that good experienced managers will be aware of without needing to see them on a document or computer screen, because they are in touch with their staff and they know their business.

Activity 19 · 15 mins

S/NVQ D1.1

This Activity may provide the basis of appropriate evidence for your S/NVQ portfolio. If you are intending to take this course of action, it might be better to write your answers on separate sheets of paper.

What information do you need in order to fulfil your responsibilities for the following, and in what form do you get it?

Allocating work day by day

What information? _____

In what form? _____

Maintaining productivity

What information? _____

In what form? _____

Controlling costs

What information? _____

In what form? _____

Planning future activities

What information? _____

In what form? _____

Seeking ways to improve productivity

What information? _____

In what form? _____

You may feel that you don't have as much information as you need. Write down what extra information you would like to have for each of the following five categories.

Allocating work day by day

_____

Maintaining productivity

_____

Controlling costs

_____

Planning future activities

_____

Seeking ways to improve productivity

_____

This activity will probably have raised a number of questions for you. Are you getting enough information? Is it accurate and reliable? Do you get it at the right time? Does it come in a form that makes sense to you? How can you improve matters?

Activity 20 · 10 mins

List the items of information that you yourself have to report regularly to your line manager or other departments of the organization. Against each one, note down what use is made of this information and what feedback you receive.

_____

_____

_____

_____

_____

2.1 Meeting your targets

All such information helps first line managers and team leaders plan their activities. However, for some purposes, a wider range of information is needed, for measuring work for example.

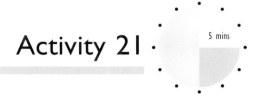

Activity 21   5 mins

You are a first line manager in charge of a team of other people. You are responsible for ensuring that they meet output and productivity targets. This means collecting information about their work.

Explain briefly what the relevant information is and how you obtain it.

_____

_____

_____

_____

Explain how you report it to your line manager and others who need to know about it.

_____

_____

The ways in which output and productivity targets are measured and recorded can vary greatly. They include the following:

■ a first line manager physically counting or measuring the output (e.g. output of letters typed, units assembled, lengths of trench dug, lines of computer code programmed);
■ self-reporting, for instance where staff submit time sheets or job sheets, or simply report back when a task is finished.

Since staff time is always a major part of total costs, there is usually a system for recording how many hours are worked, and what the pay rate per hour is. This is particularly important for measuring the cost of one-off jobs, contract work, etc.

2.2 A practical example of information needs

Let's finish this section by considering a mini case study.

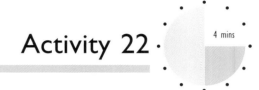

Activity 22 · 4 mins

Smita was in charge of a telephone helpline service run by a charity. Calls were answered live between 9 am and 8 pm Monday to Friday, and from 9 am to 4 pm on Saturdays. Some calls were simply for information, others were of a counselling nature, and a few constituted emergencies of some kind. Apart from Smita, all the other staff were either paid part-timers, working flexible hours, or volunteers. Smita was responsible for deploying them efficiently to ensure that enough suitably trained people were always available to cope with demand, but that costs were minimized.

What information does Smita need in order to match staff hours to caller demand efficiently? How can she get this information?

_____

_____

_____

Firstly Smita needs information about her people: she needs to know who is available when, and what their skills are. For example, staff who provide counselling must be properly trained; staff who provide information must be familiar with the information sources, and so on.

Smita may well feel that she has the information in her head about who can do what. This may work when only a handful of individuals are involved, but greater numbers will mean more information. Then it becomes necessary to have the information written down, and available at a glance. Lists, charts and rosters are probably the answer.

The other information Smita needs is about activity – in this case, demand. This varies with time of day and days of the week. Smita will certainly be aware of the broad patterns – Monday the busiest day, evenings busier than mornings, and so on. However, in order to plan her staffing efficiently she needs more detailed information.

■ She would probably need to record the number of calls of each type taken in each hourly period on each day of the week, and to build this up over several weeks.

■ She can then chart the data to show the demand patterns for a typical week.

3 Means of collecting information

Information is often collected automatically as a part of a routine activity.

■ Sensors in electronically controlled machines – from photocopiers to generator turbines – can record how many items they put out, how many times a process is repeated, how much material or energy is used, and so on.

■ Telephone systems can record what numbers were dialled at what times, for how long and at what cost.

■ Retailers' electronic tills can record large amounts of data about each transaction.

■ Travel agents and other service providers may deal with customers using computer terminals, and all the relevant data are recorded.

■ Pressure mats or light beams or sliding doors record the number of people entering a shop.

Activity 23 · 3 mins

Note down two or three situations where automatic counting of some kind would provide useful information about customer/user demand.

_____

_____

_____

Road traffic flows are an obvious example. Traffic planners can install a pressure cable across a carriageway. (The counted total of course needs to be divided by two.) Retailers need to know how many people are visiting their shops, and light beams or pressure mats can count the number of people moving past a particular point. Where entry tickets are issued, a physical or digital record can be made. Ticket machines that operate barriers in car parks collect data about the number of cars entering and leaving, and this can be used to limit access at busy times; turnstiles at leisure centres, etc. can also collect throughput data.

3.1 Big Brother?

It is increasingly common for people's work to be monitored by the equipment they are using. For example, many thousands of people work at networked computers, processing orders, invoices, inquiries etc., often dealing with sales calls direct via the phone. Their computers can be programmed to record log-on and log-off times, the number of transactions operators process and the number of errors they make. They may even be able to make voice recordings of their telephone conversations.

The electronic till and checkouts in a large retail store can record a variety of information, such as:

■ which assistant was working where;
■ the start and finish times for each session;
■ the number of transactions processed in that time;
■ the value of these transactions.

Activity 24 · 4 mins

Information that is automatically collected at sales points can be used to measure the productivity of assistants as well as providing sales and stock data.

What other information could be derived when information is collected at sales points?

_____

_____

_____

Where staff are paid by the hour, or earn commissions and bonuses on sales, sales point data can be used to help calculate them. However, the data can also be used for other purposes.

■ To analyse and compare volume and average value of sales at different sales points. This could help management decide the best locations for the sales points.

■ To reveal how sales turnover differs from day to day, and at different times of day. This will help management set staffing levels flexibly to match sales levels.

■ To identify training needs and to spot possible dishonesty. If a particular sales assistant records lower than average sales figures, irrespective of the time of day or the sales point location on which he or she is working, there is something that might need investigating. Perhaps the person needs additional training or supervision; perhaps he or she is deliberately under-recording purchases made by family and friends.

3.2 Data collection devices

Computers typically receive data input through keyboards or via communications links to other computers, but more and more different kinds of data collection device are becoming available.

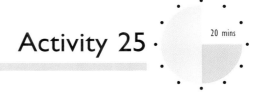

Activity 25

S/NVQ D1.1

This Activity may provide the basis of appropriate evidence for your S/NVQ portfolio. If you are intending to take this course of action it might be better to write your answers on separate sheets of paper.

Make a thorough survey of your organization, and list all the different kinds of data collection hardware that are in use. Say briefly what each is used for, and give an opinion on whether it could be used more effectively.

If you work in a very large organization, it may be impossible to investigate all areas of it, but try to cast your net as wide as possible.

Now spend some time leafing through one of the major monthly computer magazines such as *Computer Shopper, PC Direct*, etc. These magazines are not expensive, but you can probably find them in a town or college library if you don't want to buy them.

What other data collection devices are advertised or described in these magazines? Give brief details of two devices that could be of practical value to your own organization, and explain why.

_____

_____

_____

_____

_____

_____

Your answers will of course depend on what your organization does and how it functions. The general point is that IT manufacturers are steadily widening the choice of data collection and input devices, either to meet special needs or to improve efficiency.

We have already mentioned keyboards and communications links which can bring data in from the organization's internal network or from further afield.

Many other devices may be used, including:

- scratch pads on which individuals can make handwritten notes that are then converted to computer input;
- key pads, on which, for example, customers can enter PIN numbers to confirm purchases or cash withdrawals via credit card;
- credit card and smart card readers;
- bar-code readers of various types which identify the unique code printed on the product or product label;
- document scanners which can be used to digitize images and to read typed or handwritten text;
- graphics tablets, on which users can rough out a drawing or design which is then digitized;
- touch-sensitive screens;
- hand-held terminals which can store various kinds of data for transmission to the processing unit later.

Human beings collect data in ways that digital technology largely doesn't: mainly by looking and listening. Our brain power is so great, and our senses so efficient, that we can often acquire a huge amount of useful information by simply listening for a few moments or by glancing at a situation for a few seconds.

Activity 26 · 4 mins

Dalton was processing some paperwork in the office when one of the warehouse staff came in to see him. 'Mr Roberts,' said the newcomer, 'I've just been down to the cool store, and there is something that feels not quite right down there. I think you ought to check it out.'

When Dalton entered the cool store, he immediately realized that there was a slightly unusual smell in the air. He also noted something different about the sound coming from the cooling system. He called in the maintenance team, who found and replaced a faulty electric motor.

What is Dalton doing that a computer could not do?

_____

_____

_____

It is possible to fit automatic sensors to equipment and to link them to a computer that is programmed to warn staff of any deviation from the norm (no doubt the temperature in the cold store was measured in this way). But as yet there is no computer that has the quick and flexible understanding shown by Dalton and his colleague.

There is a reason for this. Human input devices (eyes, ears, nose, tongue and touch-sensitive nerve endings) are fairly basic in themselves but they are powered by a processor and memory system that is vastly bigger and more complex than anything available in a computer: the human brain.

Computer 'brains' are still puny by comparison, and their data collection systems are crude.

However, technological advances are coming ever more quickly, and there is the potential for almost anything to be an input device.

■ Voice recognition software already enables computers to interpret and respond to human speech to a limited extent and the technology is steadily improving. Voice recognition is one of the hobby horses of Microsoft supremo Bill Gates.
■ Better 'seeing' devices and software will deliver visual information in ways that computers can understand. This will enable machines to carry out surveillance, checking and inspection activities with less human supervision.

■ Smells (and to a lesser extent tastes) can now be represented in digital form – obviously useful for food and perfume manufacturers – and devices that can reproduce them are coming on to the market.

■ There is already an Internet fridge on the market which includes a touch screen and a barcode reader.

4 Storing information

If you're using electronic devices to collect information, the chances are you will store it on a computer.

How do you plan to use the information you collect? Before you make a decision about *how* to collect information, think about what you plan to do with it. It may affect how you store it. And the way you store it *may* affect the way you collect it.

In the days before computers were widely used, you had to check the card index in your local public library to find out if they had a book you wanted to borrow. The card for the book contained all its details. For example, number of copies and where to look for it on the shelves.

There were usually at least two catalogues: one ordered by author and one by classification numbers. Classification numbers are a way of organizing a collection of books by subject.

Activity 27

5 mins

Imagine you are the person who produced the information in the card catalogue. A new delivery of books has arrived and you have to get them ready to go out onto the shelves. First, you need to prepare a card for each book. How would you record the information on the card bearing in mind the needs of the borrower?

_____

_____

_____

Cards in the catalogue are laid out in a consistent way. For the author catalogue, the author is near the top, easy to find, with the last name first, followed by given names.

For the classification number catalogue, the number is the most important piece of information and it should be near the top of the card. For each catalogue, the information is laid out in the same way on every card. This makes it easy for the user to find information.

If you were the cataloguer in Activity 27, you would probably soon develop an efficient way of working. The first step is to decide which information is needed for each book. The second is to collect it as quickly as possible and in the way that makes recording it most efficient.

Method of storing affects method of collection.

4.1 Computer storage

You may store your personal information in handwritten form. An example of this is a diary. But in most workplaces these days, information is stored on a computer.

Many of the software programs available today provide ways of storing information. One example is online diaries. You can store all the information you would in a paper diary, but they offer extras, such as messages that appear on your screen reminding you that you have an appointment to go to today.

For business information, two important kinds of software that are used for storage and analysis are databases and spreadsheets. Databases are primarily for storage and spreadsheets are primarily for analysis, but it is not quite as simple as that. Either of these will store information. The best choice depends on what you want to use it for.

Over the next few pages we will spend a little time looking at the way databases and spreadsheets work.

4.2 Databases

The library catalogue in Activity 27 is a database, but we usually only call a set of information a database when it is stored on a computer.

Activity 28 · 3 mins

Can you think of any other non-computerized information you use in daily life that might be called a paper database?

_____

_____

_____

_____

_____

_____

Once you start to think about it you will probably start to see databases everywhere. Some examples are:

- dictionaries;
- telephone directories;
- address books;
- catalogues.

It may have occurred to you that many of the paper databases we have used in the past are now available on computers. Online dictionaries, telephone directories and catalogues selling clothes, furniture, food and so on, are all widely used. E-mail systems have address books where you can store e-mail addresses. Computerized information can be accessed much more quickly and amended more easily.

Where computerized records are stored in a consistent form they are referred to as databases. They are specifically designed to allow quick and easy identification and retrieval of information.

Why computerized databases?

There is additional material about using databases for storage in *Storing and Retrieving Information*.

Computerized databases have many advantages over paper versions. They usually take up less space, but a major advantage is that they allow you to find and analyse data much more easily than paper-based records.

Returning to the library catalogue: in order to be able to search using two different criteria (author and subject classification), the cataloguer had to produce two separate sets of cards. Computerized library catalogues have all the information about a book in only one database entry. You can then search for the author, the title, the subject, and any other piece of information that has been made searchable. The better the database software, the more flexibility there will be for searching – providing the person who sets it up does a good job.

Database records

A database record is a number of different pieces of information that belong together, stored as a group.

Activity 29

5 mins

Look at a mail order catalogue; any kind will do. What information is given about each item in the catalogue?

_____

_____

_____

_____

_____

_____

A catalogue item typically has:

- a unique item number;
- description;
- price;
- a picture of the item;
- sizes available (if relevant).

Depending on the type of catalogue, there may be other information, e.g. a different price for buying two or more of the same item.

It may seem strange to think of the picture as part of the database information but it is stored in the database with all the other information about the item, making a complete set.

The set of information relating to a single item is a database record. A record can contain a lot of information or just a small amount.

Using database records

How can we work with these database records?

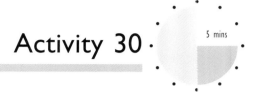

Activity 30 · 5 mins

If you were an order clerk working with a large catalogue, which pieces of information about items do you think you might find useful when searching your records to process an order?

_____

_____

_____

_____

_____

The most useful piece of information is the unique item number. This identifies the product being ordered. However, if you have completed a catalogue order form, you may have noticed that there is usually a space for a description of the item. If the product identified by the unique item number does not match up with the description, the order clerk will need to query the order.

On a computer the order in which the records are stored is not important. A computer is not like a filing cabinet where the files must be in alphabetical order. Computers search for records in a database in a different way.

Fields

Each of the individual pieces of information in a database record is stored in a _field_. You can search for the record using that piece of information. For example, suppose a school has its pupil records on a database. The teachers have noticed that pupils always come in feeling very tired after birthday parties. A search of the date of birth field produces a large number of records. It reveals that there are an unusually large number of birthdays in May. The staff can prepare for tired children.

Searching for records based on a single field may be useful, but you can also search for information contained in two or more fields. For example, all children in Class 4, whose birthdays are in May. Or you can exclude records using more than one field. For example, all children whose birthdays are in May and are *not* in Class 2.

Entering information

Records can include fields that contain text, numbers or even pictures. When setting up a database, it is vital to think about how to organize the data before you begin to enter it. Consistency of approach is the key.

If you are creating a database that will be added to by many different people, it is possible to make fields accept *only* text, or numbers or pictures. This increases the chances that the person inputting the data will put the *right* data in the field. This may not be so important for databases like online dictionaries. These are updated every so often, but do not change between updates. For a customer database, updated many times a day by different people, it can be helpful.

Analysis using databases

We saw that databases are primarily for storing data. But they are useful for certain types of analysis.

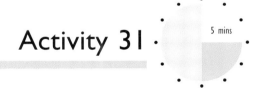

Activity 31

5 mins

A company called Al Fresco Ltd is conducting an advertising campaign for mail order garden furniture. It places adverts in a number of different kinds of publication, over a number of weeks. Customers can fill in the order coupon on the advert. Printed on the coupon is a unique code that refers to the publication and advert date. If customers order by phone, the salesperson asks for the code. All orders and customer details go onto a database.

How could Al Fresco use its information to judge the how well its marketing campaign went and to plan future campaigns?

The most basic analysis is to use the unique code to find out which publication produced the most orders. But a database can allow much more sophisticated analysis. Al Fresco could find out:

- which dates were most successful;
- whether the same dates were best for each publication;
- whether publications were more successful in particular regions.

If you have used Internet search engines, you will know that it can be very difficult to sift out the information you want from the huge number of 'hits'. This is because the information is not organized and the search engine searches through large amounts of text. You can only search a database using the searchable fields, but the information produced is 100 per cent relevant.

A well-constructed database can bring great benefits to a business both for record keeping and for business analysis. The key is to plan at the information collecting stage so that you collect the best information and record it in the most efficient and useful way.

Mail merge

Before we leave databases, we will take a look at one common way of using them to save time.

Companies like Al Fresco often want to write to all the customers on their database. Suppose they were extending a range of furniture to include a sunlounger. Al Fresco could write to all the customers who had bought that range to suggest they might like to buy a sunlounger to go with their existing furniture.

Producing a personal letter for each customer manually would be very time consuming. But sending a standard letter beginning 'Dear customer' is not such good marketing. A database can generate personalized letters automatically. You may have already come across this if you use word processors such as Microsoft Word.

- The first step is to create the standard letter you want to send. You create special fields in the places where you want to put personalized information, for example, the customer's address, and the customer's name. Al Fresco might want to mention the items from the range the customer has already purchased. For example: 'Why not add to the *two chairs* you've bought from the range already'.
- Once you have created this letter template, the word processing software can access the database fields required and produce a large number of personalized letters very quickly.

Here is an example mail merge letter for Al Fresco:

Al Fresco Ltd – Garden Furniture

The Garden Centre
Anytown

«Title»«FirstName»«LastName»
«Address1»
«Address2»

Dear «Title»«LastName»

Great news! We've updated our Mediterranean range of garden furniture. We're sure you've been enjoying the «Product» you've bought from the range already. Why not add to them with a fantastic sunlounger. Complete with comfortable cushions, and matching the rest of the range, the Mediterranean sunlounger will make your summer really special. Available to existing customers for only «Price».

Call us on «Phone» to order. Delivery within 28 days.

Call soon!

Yours sincerely

Sharon Rose
Al Fresco Ltd

Activity 32

10 mins

You work for a company that services gas boilers. Your boss has asked you to advise what fields you need in the database in order to send out a letter to each customer about a month before the annual service is due.

Make a list of the necessary fields. In a word processor produce a letter to use for mail merge. Put the names of the fields from the database in square brackets in the correct place in the letter. (You do not need to use the mail merge codes for your word processor for this exercise, although you may wish to use the online Help or the user manual to find out how to do this.)

Keep the list and the letter in a safe location on your computer. Note down where it is here:

_____

The answer to this activity is on pages 122–123.

4.3 Spreadsheets

A spreadsheet is not primarily designed for storing information. It *can* be used for storing data, but more often the information will be drawn into it from other sources, such as databases. However, when planning to collect information, think about whether you are going to analyse it using a spreadsheet. This will help you to be clearer about what information you need, how to collect it, and the form in which to store it.

What is a spreadsheet?

You have probably already come across spreadsheets. At least you may understand that they look like grids in which you type text and numbers. You may have tried to keep track of your personal spending using one.

You will need access to spreadsheet software to do the activities in this section. The activities are very basic and it is not possible to give specific instructions, since spreadsheets are all different. You may need to refer to your spreadsheet manual or online Help.

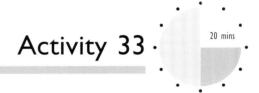

Activity 33

Create a spreadsheet that demonstrates that you have the following basic spreadsheet skills. If necessary refer to the user manual or the online Help system for your spreadsheet to find out how to do them. Print out any help pages you use.

- Enter numbers and format them, for instance make them display as 1,234 (comma format) or 5.67 (to two decimal places) or as a percentage (25% instead of 0.25).
- Enter dates such as 24/03/2004.
- Enter text.
- Select cells, copy and paste their contents and drag them to other parts of the spreadsheet.
- Sum a column of numbers.

Keep the basic skills spreadsheet file in a safe location on your computer. Note down where it is here.

Simple uses of spreadsheets

You can store and analyse simple information in a spreadsheet very easily. A good example is keeping records of monthly expenses to claim back from your employer. You could use columns to record the following information:

■ date of expense;

■ description of the expense;

■ total cost;

■ VAT, if your employer needs to know this;

■ separate categories for different types of expense, for example, mileage allowance, hotel costs, car hire, and so on.

Spreadsheets can be used for analysing management information. See the workbook *Information in Management* in this series.

At the end of the month, the spreadsheet can total all the columns automatically, and you can transfer the data onto your expenses claim form in whatever way required. Your employer might even accept a printout of a spreadsheet as a claim. Employers usually expect to see receipts and any other paper records of expenses, but for electronic storage, a spreadsheet is probably sufficient.

Inserting data from other programs

You can import data into a spreadsheet from other programs, for example, a word processor or a database. Spreadsheets let you do this in two ways:

■ You can usually copy and paste data successfully from almost anywhere.

■ If the spreadsheet you are using has a converter for the program where your data is stored, you can import a whole file.

If you are collecting information you want to analyse using a spreadsheet, take a look at how the spreadsheet allows you to import data. This may affect your method of collection. Refer to your spreadsheet's user manual or online Help for information.

Automatic calculations

One of the most useful functions of a spreadsheet is that it can perform calculations on sets of numbers automatically. The most simple is to add a set of figures. You should have found out how to do this in your spreadsheet in Activity 33.

For more complicated calculations you create a formula. The spreadsheet automatically inserts the solution to the formula in the required place.

Activity 34 ·

10 mins

In your spreadsheet create a column of about 10 to 15 numbers. Use the formula function to create a column next to it where each of the first set of numbers is multiplied by 20.

Sorting and filtering

Suppose you have a list of customers in a spreadsheet like this:

	A	B	C	D	E
1	**Name**	**Title**	**Initial**	**Address**	**Town**
2	Armitage	Mrs	P	4 High St	Bath
3	Bertram	Mr	F	6 Cedar Rd	Newcastle on Tyne
4	Deane	Miss	L	25 Norton Cres	Grimsby
5	Evans	Mr	N	42 Queens Rd	Newcastle on Tyne
6	Fuller	Mr	K	33 Seaview	Torquay
7	Harris	Mrs	O	32 Duke St	Bath
8	Ingrams	Dr	B	78 Long Rd	Maidenhead
9	Jones	Mrs	N	49 Green Rd	Aberystwyth
10	Miles	Mrs	P	3 The Avenue	Edinburgh
11	O'Brien	Miss	R	2 River View	Newcastle on Tyne
12	Pearson	Dr	A	125 Main St	Southsea
13	Smith	Miss	F	50 The Willows	Maidenhead
14	Taylor	Mrs	C	39 South St	Maidenhead
15	Watkins	Mrs	A	19 School Lane	Northampton
16	Young	Mr	A	14 Acacia Av	Preston
17					

The customers are in alphabetical order by last name. You want to target marketing at customers in a particular town. Using the sort function on your spreadsheet, you can display the customer list ordered alphabetically by town.

This groups all the customers in the same town together, like this:

	A	B	C	D	E
1	**Name**	**Title**	**Initial**	**Address**	**Town**
2	Jones	Mrs	N	49 Green Rd	Aberystwyth
3	Armitage	Mrs	P	4 High St	Bath
4	Harris	Mrs	O	32 Duke St	Bath
5	Miles	Mrs	P	3 The Avenue	Edinburgh
6	Deane	Miss	L	25 Norton Cres	Grimsby
7	Ingrams	Dr	B	78 Long Rd	Maidenhead
8	Smith	Miss	F	50 The Willows	Maidenhead
9	Taylor	Mrs	C	39 South St	Maidenhead
10	Bertram	Mr	F	6 Cedar Rd	Newcastle on Tyne
11	Evans	Mr	N	42 Queens Rd	Newcastle on Tyne
12	O'Brien	Miss	R	2 River View	Newcastle on Tyne
13	Watkins	Mrs	A	19 School Lane	Northampton
14	Young	Mr	A	14 Acacia Av	Preston
15	Pearson	Dr	A	125 Main St	Southsea
16	Fuller	Mr	K	33 Seaview	Torquay
17					

If you have a large number of customers and want to display only the customers living in, say, Newcastle on Tyne, you can use the spreadsheet's filter facility to filter out customers living everywhere else. This is the result:

	A	B	C	D	E
1	**Name** ▾	**Tit** ▾	**Initi** ▾	**Address** ▾	**Town** ▾
10	Bertram	Mr	F	6 Cedar Rd	Newcastle on Tyne
11	Evans	Mr	N	42 Queens Rd	Newcastle on Tyne
12	O'Brien	Miss	R	2 River View	Newcastle on Tyne
17					

Graphics

Spreadsheets can also convert data into graphic formats: bar charts, line graphs and pie charts. These can be useful ways of analysing data. You may notice a trend in a graphic that isn't obvious from a set of figures in a table.

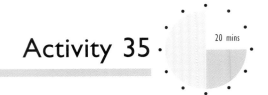

Activity 35

20 mins

Create an imaginary set of expenses for a month in your spreadsheet. Include costs for mileage, hotel bills and meals. Refer to the user manual or the online Help for your spreadsheet to help you create a pie chart, showing the proportion of total expenses for each of the three kinds of expense.

Keep the spreadsheet in a safe location on your computer. Note down where it is here:

_____

Spreadsheets and databases are very useful tools. You can use them to store and analyse data for any number of different purposes. It is worth thinking about whether you will be using either of them, and to plan your information collection process accordingly.

5 Questioning techniques

In spite of all these developments there will often be occasions when the best way of collecting information is to talk to people and ask them questions.

- You will often do this when you are having meetings with your team as a whole or with individual members.
- You may need to discuss a problem with people from other departments in the organization, or find out what they expect of you.
- If customers call you or visit your premises you may need to ask them a series of questions before you fully understand the nature of their query and know how to answer it.
- You may be involved in market research activities.

Obviously you know what a question is, and how to ask one, but if you sometimes struggle to get the answers you need, you may like to give some thought to your questioning technique.

Broadly speaking there are two types of question: open and closed. Either may be appropriate for gathering information, depending on the circumstances, or it may be best to use a combination.

5.1 Closed questions

Closed questions give people a choice of predetermined answers or can simply be answered with a 'Yes' or 'No' or a tick in a box or a very short factual answer. In conversation and information gathering they help to establish the basic facts.

Title   Mr ☐   Mrs ☐   Miss ☐   Ms ☐   Dr ☐   Other ☐

Would you like a sales representative to call you?	Yes ☐	No ☐

The advantage is that you will get short, relevant answers that are easy to analyse.

The disadvantage is that the choices may be too restrictive to cover every possibility.

Written **questionnaires** are usually made up mainly of closed questions: we'll discuss questionnaires in more detail in a moment.

Leading questions

Leading questions prompt the person you are questioning with the expected reply. 'Wouldn't you agree that ...?' or 'We are particularly interested in recruiting people with strong communication skills. Are you good on the telephone?'

Obviously the problem with this type of question is that people are likely to give the answer that they think you want to hear.

There is sometimes a case for using a leading question if the person you are questioning is reluctant to talk.

5.2 Open questions

Open questions let people respond in their own words. Typically an open question begins with 'Why ...?' or 'How ...?' or a phrase like 'Could you describe ...' or 'Tell me more about ...'.

The advantage of this type of question is that it is less likely to lead people into giving the answer they think you want to hear.

The disadvantage is that you may end up collecting a large amount of subjective data. This may or may not be relevant, and you will need to spend time reading and interpreting it to find out.

Activity 36

4 mins

Here are two questions and the answers that were received.

Q1: What colour is your car?

A1: It's a blue Jaguar XJS convertible . . . 5.3 litre . . . H reg, but it's only done 30,000 miles. Bit expensive to run, but lovely in the summer . . .

Q2: What colour are the walls in your living room?

A2: Sea Thistle

Assuming these were not the kind of answers you were looking for, what is wrong with the questions?

_____

_____

_____

_____

The answer to this activity is on page 123.

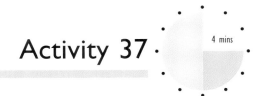

Activity 37

4 mins

Rewrite the following closed questions as open questions.

Would you prefer rice or pasta?

_____

Do you enjoy your job?

_____

Are you going away at the weekend or staying at home?

_____

Our suggested answers are on page 123.

Probing questions

Probing questions are open questions that follow up something mentioned in a previous answer and ask for more details. For example, 'You say your computer keeps crashing. What are you doing immediately before the crashes?'

Problem-solving questions

Problem-solving questions set up a brief scenario and ask people how they would deal with it. ('You have a customer on the phone and she is being abusive because the product she ordered has not arrived. How would you calm her down and how would you deal with her complaint?')

These sorts of question can be useful in recruitment interviews and staff appraisals, when you want to know whether the other person has adequate technical knowledge to deal with problems that are likely to occur in the job, or you want to know more about their attitudes. They can also be useful for generating new ideas.

Friendly Martian

This is a useful technique for getting a fresh perspective on a situation and making sure that nothing is taken for granted. It may help to encourage people to talk in situations where they are assuming that you already have as much knowledge as they do, or when you want to check their detailed understanding. Again, it may also help to generate new ideas.

You would ask the person to explain something (how to reply to a letter, say) as if they were talking to someone who has just arrived from another planet, covering all the things the alien should do or should not do.

For instance you could not simply say '... then post the letter': you would have to explain exactly how this works, because the Martian would have no knowledge of envelopes or stamps or franking machines, out trays, post boxes, the mail service, and so on.

5.3 Steering the conversation

A useful technique to ensure that you get the information you require, and only the information you require, is to think of people's knowledge in terms of a system of folders and sub-folders, like a computer file manager.

Suppose you worked for a company that specialized in holidays on some of the smaller, less well-known Greek Islands and you were asked to conduct research on people's views. Rather than just launching into the topic ('Good afternoon, madam, have you ever been to Skyros?') the following approach may get you a better response.

Good morning, would you mind answering a few questions? I'm conducting a survey on people's holiday preferences.	Closed question to open the Holidays folder in the person's mind
Do you take holidays during the summer?	Closed question to open the Summer Holiday sub-folder. (You are not interested in their skiing holidays.)
And would you usually go abroad?	Closed question to open the Holidays Abroad sub-folder
Which countries have you visited? (or list the countries you want to know about)	Respondent lists the folders: Bahamas, Spain, etc.
Ah, now Greece. Tell me more about ...	Open questions begin here and the respondent is now fully focussed on the topic you want to know about.

With a little imagination this technique can be adapted to almost any situation. Try it next time you are talking to someone who is inclined to ramble off the topic!

5.4 Listening to the answer

If you want people to give you information then you need to pay some attention to the way you ask questions and how you listen. Questions should be paced and put carefully. Your manner and tone of voice, and the way questions are phrased, particularly early on in a conversation, can all affect the willingness of people to talk to you and the ease with which they do so. Here are some useful rules.

- Avoid confusing or intimidating the person by plunging immediately into demanding questions or picking up on small points.
- Avoid the temptation to talk too much yourself.
- Allow the other person to ask questions.
- Don't allow the person to gloss over important points if those are the ones you are particularly interested in.
- Do not let your own attitudes or prejudices get in the way.
- Be aware of the **halo effect** – the tendency to judge people and what they say based on personal characteristics, such as being neatly dressed, or well-spoken.
- **Avoid stereotyping** by attributing certain characteristics to a group as a whole (graduates, women, people from Birmingham, say), and then assuming that each individual member of the supposed group will possess that characteristic: 'women know nothing about cars'; 'graduates have no common sense', and so on.
- Listen to and evaluate the responses so that you get the information you want.
- Listen to what the person wants to say, but if it isn't what you need to know steer the conversation in the right direction as quickly as possible.
- Listen out for what the person is trying *not* to say. Are you only getting the answers the person thinks you want to hear?
- Listen to what the person is saying, but doesn't mean, or is lying about.
- Listen to what the person is having difficulty saying.

5.5 Example: questioning techniques

Activity 38

20 mins

Suppose you are in charge of Workteam A and you provide a service to Workteam B. You want to find out whether there is any more you and your team can do to satisfy the needs of the other team.

How would you go about this? What questioning techniques would you use?

_____

_____

_____

_____

_____

_____

_____

_____

Here are some brief suggestions. You probably had additional ideas.

Decide who to ask

Do you only ask the manager of Workteam B, do you seek the views of individual members of the team, or do you ask the whole team in a meeting?

Obviously it is courteous to ask the manager in the first instance and he or she will almost certainly have a broader perspective than individual members.

You could follow this up with a written questionnaire for everyone in Workteam B and, once those results were analysed, with a meeting involving the manager and several members of the team to follow up issues raised in more detail.

Prepare your questions

The meeting with the manager would probably be largely unstructured with a single question ('What more can Workteam A do to satisfy the needs of Workteam B?') and a wide ranging discussion.

The group meeting would be far more structured, perhaps with an outline agenda and a time limit.

Control the meeting

You might begin the meeting with a closed question that simply presented people with a list of things that your workteam does for them and get them to agree that that is what you do (or not). Easy questions that provoke little disagreement will help to get the discussion going.

Note that you would need to do some advance preparation of hand-outs or PowerPoint slides.

Then you can move on to a more open-ended question asking for opinions on how well your team does in each of the areas that have been identified. You could perhaps ask for anecdotal evidence: people find it easier to tell stories about things that have actually happened than to generalize.

The next open question would ask 'What would you like us to do better or do differently?' This may already have arisen during the previous discussion, but if not it is important to ask the question. The friendly Martian technique could be helpful here.

Finally you might ask another open question: 'What else would you like us to do that we don't do already?' However, there's a good chance that if you ask the question in this way you will get no response at all.

A variation on the friendly Martian technique is to use a third party: 'If you were paying an outside company to do this for you would you try to get more for your money? What sort of extras would you expect from them?' The idea is that people will feel more comfortable if they don't have to criticize you directly.

6 Questionnaires, surveys and observation

Questionnaires and surveys are fairly similar things. The term 'questionnaire' is most often used to describe a written document that the respondents fill in themselves, whereas a 'survey' is conducted by asking people the questions face-to-face or on the telephone.

Observation, obviously, means watching and noting down what happens, but not interacting with the people that make it happen.

6.1 Questionnaire design

EXTENSION 3
Questionnaire Design by Alan Oppenheim gives valuable tips on this topic.

Questionnaires are a useful way of gathering relatively small amounts of information from a lot of people. However, it is much more difficult than you might think to create a really good questionnaire.

The key is to make it as easy as possible for people to fill in the questionnaire and as easy as possible for you to analyse the answers. But it is very hard to know, in advance, what it is that you might like to know, and it is even harder to predict all the possible answers – if you could do that, why bother with a questionnaire?

For instance, suppose you design a questionnaire with the following (open) question and put a large blank box underneath for the answer.

What method(s) of communication did you use the last time you arranged to meet someone or a group of other people?

Some people would simply write or type 'phone and e-mail', but (depending on the size of the blank box) others may be tempted to scribble you a little story about what the event was, who was there, how the initial idea for the event was a spontaneous conversation in the kitchen at work, how the news spread like wildfire by phone and e-mail, and so on – all of which you would have to decipher, read and interpret, but almost all of which you do not need to know!

A much better way to get the information you want is to offer a limited range of possible responses to the question, something along these lines.

Please indicate what methods of communication you used the last time you arranged to meet someone or a group of other people

(☑ *Tick all boxes that apply*)

E-mail	☐	I do not meet other people	☐
Telephone conversation	☐	Message pinned on notice board	☐
Post	☐	Website/chatroom	☐
Text message	☐	Face-to-face	☐

Other (please give brief details)

....

....

The answers to this (almost closed) question will be much easier to analyse, and it will be much quicker for people to answer the question if they do not have to think up their own words.

So far as possible you should avoid putting the choices in the order that you think reflects their popularity: note the two column layout, which tries to avoid this.

Note that the text and the associated boxes to tick are closely aligned and shaded so that it is crystal clear which box belongs to which option.

It is also clear in this example that you want a tick, not a cross. Actually it probably doesn't matter what mark people use, but remember that lots of people are scared of forms: save them from worrying and make it crystal clear for them.

If the answer is 'Other' it is clear from the wording and the limited space for the answer that you do not want much detail.

Activity 39

3 mins

Suppose you were analysing the responses to the above questionnaire and got an answer under 'Other' saying 'Silent hand signal indicating 'drinking a pint'', plus quizzically raised eyebrow'.

How would you include this in your results?

_____

_____

_____

Our answer to this activity is on page 123.

Here are some further guidelines on questionnaire design.

Explain and give instructions

People are always happier to give information, and they will give you better information, if they understand why you want it. So include a brief introduction explaining the purpose of the questionnaire and how the information will be used. This is often done by stressing the potential benefits to people who answer: 'Thank you for helping us to help you to . . .'.

Don't forget to make it clear what people should do with the questionnaire when they have completed it. You may wish to include a date by which it should be returned. Give a return address, preferably free of postage charges: either give a FREEPOST address or include a pre-paid, pre-addressed envelope.

Give clear instructions on how to answer the questions. Capital letters are usually easier to read, and dark (black or blue) ink is easier to photocopy or scan by computer. As mentioned already, you should also make it clear what format should be used for the answers – ticks or crosses, say, or a specific date format.

Activity 40

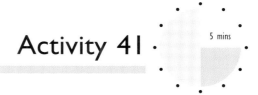

3 mins

What is wrong with this extract from a questionnaire?

Date of purchase: | | | | | | |

The answer to this question is on page 123.

Assure anonymity

Questionnaires issued to the general public should not usually ask people for personal details at all and they should assure people that any answers they give are given in strictest confidence. You have certain legal obligations here: see the final part of this session.

Activity 41

5 mins

You have issued a questionnaire to your workteam and have assured them that any answers they give are given anonymously and in strictest confidence. But one of the responses you have received is highly critical of you, and you recognize the handwriting. What should you do?

There isn't an easy answer to this question. We've suggested a way forward on page 124.

Say thank you (and/or offer rewards)

At the end of any questionnaire (or in advance in the introduction) you should thank people for taking the time and trouble to fill it in. Sometimes you may need to go further and offer some incentive for filling in and returning the questionnaire: a prize draw, say, or vouchers.

Know what you want to know

Make sure that the questions will provide all the information you require. For example you might ask people which computer platform they use and give them the choice of Windows, Apple Mac or Unix/Linux. However, you will still not know how many use, say, Windows 98 as opposed to Windows XP. You will regret this if you later discover that the software you want to sell them will only work with Windows XP or Mac OS X.

Keep it as short as possible

Most people will be happy to answer a few well-designed questions but will quickly get bored if the questionnaire is too long. It should be as short and quick to complete as possible.

This is also important for analysis of the completed questionnaires. Use as few sides of paper as possible, and bear in mind that single or double-sided sheets are easier to handle than folded or stapled sheets. In addition folds and staples will make it impossible to scan the questionnaires and read the responses into a computer.

Make it easy

Think carefully about the intended audience for the questionnaire, and make sure that the questions are worded in a way that those people will understand. Long words and complex sentences should be avoided. So should technical terms unless you know for certain that the people who receive the questionnaire will understand them.

Also bear in mind that if people have to spend time looking things up they probably won't bother. For instance if you ask people the year of registration of their car many won't know: they will only know that it is an 'X reg', say, and actually this is all the information you need from them (you can look it up yourself).

Avoid calculations

Questions that ask people to perform calculations are troublesome because people might get the calculations wrong. If possible it is better to give a list of options or ask for the figures and do the calculation yourself as part of the analysis of completed questionnaires.

Above all, test it!

It is essential to pilot test your questionnaire. Mistakes, ambiguities and omitted questions can be very costly. Ideally you should try the questionnaire out on people similar to the intended audience, though this may not always be possible. Analyse the results of the test very carefully to see if you are getting the information you need.

Here are the key things to consider about each question in your questionnaire.

- Is the question really necessary?
- Is it a leading question that encourages people to give a particular answer?
- Will people find the question too personal or be offended by it?
- Is it ambiguous? In other words could different people interpret it in different ways? For example, if you ask 'Which methods of public transport do you use regularly?' the word 'regularly' could be interpreted very differently by different people.

6.2 Surveys

By 'survey' we mean a structured interview conducted face-to-face, usually in shopping centres or door-to-door, or else voice-to-voice over the telephone. In other words a survey is like a questionnaire except that the interviewer reads out the question and fills in the answer. Much of what we have said already about questionnaire design also applies to surveys.

Surveys have a number of advantages over a questionnaire that is just sent out in the post. For example:

- the interviewer can check that the person is 'suitable' before beginning the interview: the right age or sex or salary range, say;
- response rates are higher: interviewers can continue to interview people until they reach their quota;
- this approach ensures that all questions will be answered;
- the interviewer can make sure that the person understands the question and that the answer contains the information required;
- there is more scope for open questions.

Naturally, there are also some disadvantages:

■ surveys are more expensive than questionnaires because you need to employ and train interviewers;

■ interviewers may influence the answers that are given, especially if they themselves don't understand the questions or the information required;

■ interviewers may create the wrong mood: for example if they take a very light-hearted approach the person they are interviewing may not give serious answers.

6.3 Observation

Observation is sometimes a useful way of cross-checking information you have obtained by other means such as a survey or questionnaire. Sometimes people will say, and genuinely believe, one thing when something else is actually true.

For instance staff may say that they do a task one way (perhaps because that is what they think managers want to hear) but do it quite differently in reality.

There are one or two things to consider when designing an observation exercise.

■ Will the observation be open, so that the people or persons being watched can see the observer, or will it be disguised in some way. Disguised observation is often done by closed circuit TV these days.

■ Is any special equipment needed? You may need a stopwatch or a tally counter, or something more sophisticated such as a handheld computer or scanner.

■ Will the observation be structured (in other words the observer decides what to observe in advance) or unstructured (for instance when it is impossible to predict in advance what will happen). The best approach may be to carry out unstructured observation initially and then draw up a checklist and carry out more extensive structured observation later.

Observation is most suitable when:

■ the activity or behaviour is visible. Obviously feelings, beliefs and attitudes can't be accurately judged simply by watching people;

■ the activity or behaviour is something that is done frequently or repeatedly and only takes a short time.

Observation has the advantage that it places no reliance on people's knowledge, memories, or honesty. However, it is not always possible or feasible, and it may be very labour intensive because there is a limit to how much a single observer can observe. You also have to bear in mind that people often behave differently from normal if they know they are being watched.

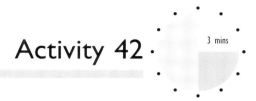

Activity 42   3 mins

You are probably well aware of roadside cameras monitoring traffic flow (and speeding), but if you keep your eyes open when you are out and about on foot you will often see data being collected by physical observation. Watch out for examples and note them here next time you see this.

_____

_____

_____

7 Constraints on data collection

There are a few constraints on **collecting** information.

- Sometimes people will just refuse to tell you what you want to know – and they will be perfectly within their rights to do so.
- Sometimes people may be unwilling to give you information unless you pay them for it. For instance, you cannot view the full contents of many journals and magazines online unless you subscribe to the magazine.
- Some information is subject to the Official Secrets Act and you will not be allowed to look at it. Commercial organizations may guard parts of their information in a similar way, for instance the recipe for Coca Cola.
- Some information is 'personal', and organizations are prevented from allowing you to collect it without asking the permission of the individual in question.

It is perhaps more accurate to say that there are constraints on **storing** information and **using** information, less so on collecting it. But presumably, if you collect information you will need to store it and you intend to use it!

7.1 The Data Protection Act 1998

EXTENSION 4
The full details of the Data Protection Act are available on the Internet.

The Data Protection Act 1998 is concerned with 'personal data', which is information about living, identifiable individuals. This can be as little as a name and address: it need not be particularly sensitive information. If it is sensitive (explained later) then extra care is needed.

The Act gives individuals certain rights, and it requires those who collect and use personal information to be open about their use of that information and to follow 'sound and proper practices' (the data protection principles).

The eight data protection principles cover matters such as whether the personal information is used for legitimate purposes, whether it is accurately recorded, and whether it is kept securely (not given out to anyone who happens to phone up, for example).

The Data Protection Act 1998 is described in more detail in another workbook in this series: *Storing and Retrieving Information*

You should be particularly aware of 'sensitive' data, especially if you are collecting information from people via interview or questionnaire. If you collect sensitive personal data it is likely that you need the explicit consent of the individual concerned.

These are the eight categories of sensitive information:

■ the racial or ethnic origin of data subjects;
■ their political opinions;
■ their religious beliefs or other beliefs of a similar nature;
■ whether they are members of a trade union;
■ their physical or mental health or condition;
■ their sexual life;
■ the commission or alleged commission by them of any offence;
■ any details of court proceedings or sentences against them.

As a rule you should ask yourself whether you actually need information of this nature, not collect it just because you can.

7.2 Copyright

EXTENSION 5
Understanding Copyright by Graham Cornish gives more information on this complex area.

Copyright law is highly specialized, so we are only going to consider matters that it might be useful to know for day-to-day office work or which are of general interest.

Copyright is a way of ensuring that the creators of a work have an exclusive right to use it, and also have the right to stop others from using the work without their permission.

Copyright can be owned by an individual, a group, or an organization.

There is no need for an author to register copyright with anybody. Usually publishers will mark the work with the international copyright symbol ©, but this is not actually necessary: copyright applies as soon as the material is 'recorded' (in writing, on a cassette tape, on a computer screen, etc.) as opposed to just being in the creator's brain.

Here are the key points that you should be aware of.

■ The main legislation in the UK is The Copyright, Designs and Patents Act 1988 (CDPA 1988), which covers the following types of 'work':

  ■ original 'literary' works, which means published materials of all kinds, including text in newspapers, books, magazines, marketing brochures and websites;
  ■ short stories, poems, words of songs, dramatic works;
  ■ musical works;
  ■ images, paintings, drawings, photographs, pottery, sculpture, and so on;
  ■ sound recordings, films, broadcasts and cable programmes;
  ■ computer programs;

■ most other countries have similar legislation. This is particularly relevant if you are using material from the Internet;
■ copyright generally applies for a period of 70 years from the end of the calendar year in which the author dies (The Duration of Copyright and Rights in Performances Regulations 1995);
■ copyright covers the **form** or **expression** of an idea, not the idea itself: it covers the way the words or notes or visual images are arranged, not what they convey.

For example, if you pick up some new ideas about doing your job from this book you can't be prevented from discussing those ideas with your workteam in a meeting.

However, if you copy paragraphs from this book and try to publish them in your own book without the permission of the publishers or author of this book, you are infringing copyright and could be sued for damages.

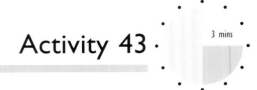

Activity 43

3 mins

In what sense is a computer program the 'expression of an idea'?

The answer to this Activity is given on page 124.

For the purpose of gathering information you should be aware that under CPDA 1988 copying includes **storing** the copyright work in any medium by electronic means. (Many websites include their own notification that gives you permission to download pages and store them on your computer for, perhaps, 30 days.)

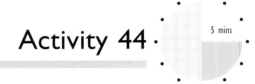

Activity 44

5 mins

Visit the BBC's website and read the Terms and Conditions in full. Get into the habit of doing this for any other website that you visit regularly.

Exceptions

There are certain provisions in CPDA 1988 relating to the use of short passages, and the use of material for educational purposes or private research. But, contrary to popular belief, there are NO exceptions to this that you can safely rely on. So:

- it is NOT allowable to copy material if you just use a sentence or two;
- it is NOT allowable if you are only using the material for educational purposes.

If there is a dispute the **courts** will consider the issue of **'fair dealing'** (section 29 and following, CPDA 1988), and this will be different in every case. The **person copying the material cannot decide** what is fair use. Case law about this is far more developed in the USA than in the UK.

7.3 Photocopying

It is normally permissible to photocopy a few pages of someone else's work for research (either commercial or non-commercial) or private study, but again this is subject to the notion of 'fair dealing'.

It is not considered fair, for example, to make a single copy of a **whole** book (even if it is only a short one), or to make lots of copies of extracts from a book to circulate to every member of your team, say, or to a class of pupils.

The use of photocopying for educational purposes is limited to 1% of a work in every three months, unless a licensing agreement has been entered into with the publisher and author.

7.4 Letters and other works written by you

If you write a **private** letter, **you** own the copyright. The recipient is not entitled to publish it without your permission (unless you write to somebody that normally publishes readers' letters, like a newspaper). This also applies to your **e-mails** or postings on an Internet noticeboard.

If, in the course of your **job,** you write something (a letter, a report, a training programme, and so on) you have created it for your employer, and **your employer** almost certainly owns the copyright.

The same normally applies to any other 'work' you create as part of your job (for instance a word processor macro), unless you have an agreement to the contrary.

Self-assessment 2

15 mins

1   List three types of information you might need when allocating work.

_____

_____

_____

2   What is self-reporting?

_____

_____

3   What items of information might be logged automatically about the work of someone using a computer on a network?

_____

_____

4   List five types of computer-linked data collection device.

_____

_____

_____

_____

5   What is a field in a database?

_____

_____

6   What spreadsheet function can you use to display a subset of all the data in a file?

_____

_____

7   What is the difference between a closed question and an open question?

_____

_____

8   What should you try to detect when listening to the answer to a question?

_____

_____

9   Apart from keeping it short and easy, and testing it, summarize two other things you should attend to when designing a questionnaire.

_____

_____

10   When is observation a suitable method for collecting information?

_____

_____

11   List three types of 'sensitive' information under the Data Protection Act 1998.

_____

_____

_____

12   Copyright legislation prevents you from re-using other people's ideas. True or False? Explain your answer.

_____

_____

Answers to these questions can be found on page 119–121.

7 Summary

- The information you need depends on the work that you and your workteam do, what resources you need to do it, and what is expected of you. It will be information to help you allocate work, monitor progress, deal with problems, plan for the future, and so on.

- Information is often collected automatically using sensors, pressure mats, computer logging and the like. There are many computerized data collection and input devices besides the basic keyboard and mouse. Examples include bar code readers, hand-held computers and scratch pads, credit card readers, and so on.

- The technology is steadily developing and we are likely to see improved voice recognition software and perhaps devices that can see and smell.

- Before collecting information it is a good idea to think about how you will store it and analyse it. This may well affect the *way* you go about collecting it.

- Databases are used for storing information in a systematic way on a computer. They allow you to search for and access your information in a very flexible way.

- Spreadsheets are primarily an analysis tool, although you may want to use them to store small amounts of information ready for analysis. They can help you to monitor all aspects of business by producing reports in different formats, including graphic.

- Questions fall into two basic types: closed questions and open questions, and there are various sub-categories of open question such as probing questions and problem-solving questions.

- A key part of asking questions is listening to the answers you get.

- Questionnaires are useful for gathering relatively small amounts of information, but they can be very difficult to design. The key is to make them as easy as possible to fill in and analyse. Most of the questions should be closed questions. It is vitally important to test a questionnaire before issuing it to the target audience.

- Surveys have certain advantages over questionnaires, especially when you want to ask open questions. However, they are more expensive, and bad interviewers can distort the results.

- Observation can sometimes be a useful way of capturing information about activities or behaviour. Again it is fairly labour intensive, and people may not behave in their normal way if they know they are being watched.

- The Data Protection Act places constraints on what personal data you can collect, store and re-use about individuals. In particular you should be careful about 'sensitive data' such as political opinions, health matters, and so on.

- Copyright law places constraints on whether you can store and re-use most types information in its original form. The creators of a work have an exclusive right to use it, and also have the right to stop others from using the work without their permission.

Session C
The Internet

1 Introduction

As we said in Session A, the **Internet** is the richest secondary source of information of all – on any subject you can think of and many that you would never think of.

It is almost certain that you will have used the Internet to gather information already, though possibly not for work purposes.

- If you have external e-mail you use that part of the Internet all the time to collect information from the people you deal with, including friends.
- If you have internal e-mail you use Internet technology to exchange information with colleagues and issue and receive instructions.
- You may have downloaded mp3 files or games for leisure purposes.
- You may have found cheap flights or holidays via the Internet.
- You may do your banking online.
- You may have followed up a link that someone else told you about (for instance in an e-mail).

Most of this session assumes you have some familiarity with the Internet, but section 2 takes you through the basics just in case you haven't. We then move on to the usual search methods – search engines, and so on – and spend some time discussing how you can improve your searching abilities and gather better information. Finally there are a few words about intranets and about Internet abuse and how to deal with it.

2 Internet basics

You can probably just skim read this section if you already use the Internet.

2.1 Internet Service Providers (ISPs)

Connection to the Internet is usually made via an Internet Service Provider (ISP) such as Freeserve or America Online (AOL) for home users, or perhaps Demon or Claranet or UUNet for businesses. If you access the Internet at work you may not be aware of the ISP at all.

Increasingly, it is possible to access the Internet via other devices such as mobile phones and televisions, but for work purposes you are most likely to use your computer.

2.2 Browsers and e-mail

Most people use the Internet through interface programs called **browsers** that make it more user-friendly and accessible. The most popular and best known, with about 95% of all users, is **Microsoft Internet Explorer**. (The remaining 5% of users use Mozilla, Netscape Navigator, which is based on Mozilla, or Opera.)

Strictly speaking, what you usually see when you use a browser is the **World Wide Web**, which is only part of the Internet.

Another part of the Internet that you are likely to use very often is its **e-mail** services, usually accessed by a program called an 'e-mail client'. The most popular is Microsoft Outlook (or Outlook Express for home users).

E-mail is covered in much more detail in another workbook in this series: *Writing Effectively*.

There are several other ways of using the Internet to connect to computers in other locations, such as **Telnet**. You will probably never use this unless it happens to be part of your job to do so.

2.3 Accessing the Internet

It should be no more difficult to get on to the World Wide Web, once your computer is set up to do so, than it is to start up any other program.

You will probably find an icon on your computer for an Internet Service Provider such as Freeserve or America Online (AOL) or simply a browser such as Microsoft Internet Explorer. All you have to do to get started is **double-click** on the icon.

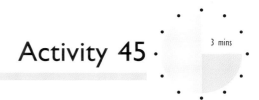

Activity 45

3 mins

If necessary, check with the IT department in your organization and find out what you need to do to get access to the Internet. Depending how your system is set up you may need to supply a user name and a password. Your system administrator will advise you about this too.

Make a note here for future reference.

_____

_____

_____

_____

If this is not possible within your organization, you may need to do this via a home computer or within a college or learning environment.

2.4 Site navigation

Once you reach a site it will usually be clear how to find your way around it, assuming the site is reasonably well designed.

If you ever get lost in a site you can sometimes click on the site logo (usually in the top left-hand corner) or 'Home' button to get back to the home page and start again.

Sometimes there will be a series of buttons or underlined links that you can click on, probably on the left, as shown below.

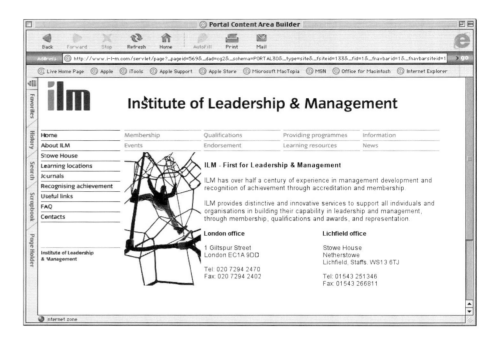

Another often-used design is the 'menu' type, as in the next example. Note that all the menu links are also reproduced as simple text links at the foot of the page.

There are all sorts of variations on these basic themes.

Activity 46

4 mins

Look at the illustration of the home page of the Inland Revenue site below. How many different methods of navigation can you see and what are they?

© Crown copyright 2002

The Inland Revenue site has menu navigation links at the top and left side of the page, a set of 'Go' boxes on the right that take you quickly to a specific page, a full index (often called a site map) that would allow you to see all the pages on the site at a glance, a number of specially featured pages, and also some simple text links at the foot of the page.

Unfortunately, there are lots of sites that do not follow basic good design principles and if you find yourself using one it can be very frustrating. If information is available from a number of sites, it is best to choose the well-designed ones that let you navigate easily through the information displayed. Don't spend a lot of time at an unsatisfactory website – look elsewhere if possible.

2.5 Favourites

If you find a site that is particularly useful to you, you do not have to do a fresh search for it every time you want to consult it again. Browsers have an option to save a list of 'favourites' for future use.

This can be very useful, but it is best to use it fairly sparingly, otherwise you will quickly end up with a list that is so long it is unmanageable: you will spend longer scouring your list than you would doing a fresh search.

2.6 Plug-ins and other software

Sooner or later in your Web explorations you will also come across 'zip' files or archives, which are compressed to make them quicker to download to your computer. To uncompress them for reading you need one of the free unzipping programs such as Winzip (http://www.winzip.com/) or PkZip (http://www.pkware.com/).

Some websites require additional 'plug-ins' to view their live content. A plug-in is simply a program that adds additional functionality to your browser. The best known are Macromedia Flash and Adobe Acrobat, though there are numerous others. If you try to look at Web content that requires a plug-in that you do not have you will usually be prompted to download and install it.

Flash is a very widely used technology for Web animations. Flash support is built in to modern browsers, so you may not even be aware that you are looking at Flash content.

Adobe Acrobat is a program that is used to create 'pdf' files that can be viewed and printed exactly as they were created (the same fonts, colours, layout, and so on) no matter what computer you use to look at them. All you need is the free **Acrobat Reader** available for download from the Adobe site (http://www.adobe.com). Again, pdf files are very widely used, especially on government sites, so it is well worth getting the Reader.

3 Searching the Internet

EXTENSION 6
Niall O'Dochartaigh's
*Internet Research
Handbook* is a useful
guide.

There are a number of ways to access information on the Internet:

- go directly to a site, if you have the address;
- browse or surf;
- explore a subject directory or portal;
- conduct a search using a search engine;
- explore information stored in live databases on the Web, known as the 'invisible web' or the 'deep web'.

At the time of publication of this book the distinctions between directories, search engines, and so on are becoming increasingly blurred, as each type of search tool picks up and adopts ideas from its competitors.

3.1 Going directly to an Internet address (URL)

EXTENSION 7
Some suggested useful
websites are listed here.

You may know the precise address of an Internet site that you wish to visit. TV and radio programmes and advertisements frequently give you a Web address to visit to find more information. You will also see addresses in newspapers, magazines and books. You may be sent a link in an e-mail.

Typically the format is something like **'http://www.bbc.co.uk'**. This is also known as a Uniform Resource Locator, or URL for short.

All you need to do is type the URL into the Address box of your browser (you can almost always omit the http:// part, if you wish) and click on Go.

Activity 47 · 5 mins

Up-to-date versions of Microsoft Internet Explorer and Netscape Navigator can sometimes find the precise site you are looking for if you just type a 'guess' directly in the address box. For instance if you just type 'boots.com' or 'sainsbury.co.uk' in the address box your browser should find the sites of these high street stores (even if the site has a rather different name from the company itself).

Try this with four or five other well-known organizations and see what results you get.

Can you see any drawbacks to this method of finding sites?

_____

_____

_____

We don't recommend this approach because it is too haphazard, as you have probably discovered, having tried this Activity.

The main drawback is that you usually need to guess the second part of the address (.com, .co.uk, .org, .net, and so on): it may take several goes before you get it right, in which case it would have been quicker to use a proper search tool such as the ones described below.

3.2 Browsing or surfing

Random browsing of pages on the Web is another haphazard way of collecting information, although it can be very interesting if you are not pressed for time.

For instance you may visit a particular news site regularly and find that an article contains links to other pages, either within that site or on an external site that contain more information about the topic. To see this in action find an article of interest to you at http://www.bbc.co.uk and follow up some of the external links.

3.3 Directories and portals

Directories

A directory is a service that offers links to Web pages organized into subject categories. Directory services supposedly contain links only to pages that have been evaluated by human beings, using various selection criteria, though the selectivity varies among services.

The best known example of a directory is Yahoo (http://www.yahoo.com), although Yahoo does not evaluate sites as carefully as some other directories and it is aimed more at the leisure interests of home computer users than at the serious academic or business researcher.

Most directories also include some kind of search facility which either searches the directory only or (confusingly) searches the Web in general, perhaps using another type of search tool. Yahoo searches, for instance, are powered by the Google search engine (described below), so Yahoo is actually a mixture between a directory and a search engine.

The best subject directories include notes about sites written by independent reviewers, describing and evaluating site content. For instance you would probably find a site such as the Social Science Information Gateway (SOSIG) (http://www.sosig.ac.uk) far more informative about useful business-related sites than Yahoo.

Portals

A **portal** is similar to a directory (and the terms are often used interchangeably) but many portals are much narrower in scope, restricting their links to specific subjects. Examples include www.thisislondon.co.uk (for Londoners!) and www.fool.com (for investors) or, more generally, the home pages of most of the leading ISPs such as Virgin and Freeserve.

Vortals

Yet another term you may see used is **vortal** (vertical industry portal) which is a portal providing information and resources for a particular industry. Examples include
www.accountingweb.co.uk and
www.privatehealth.co.uk
among thousands of others.

Typical services offered by portal or vortal sites include a directory of related websites, a facility to search for other sites, news, and community services such as discussion boards and suppliers' directories.

3.4 Search engines

Search engines such as AltaVista or Google retrieve links to, and brief descriptions of, websites containing a word or phrase entered by the user. The descriptions are derived from the webpage itself: there is no human judgement involved other than the judgement of the original author of the page.

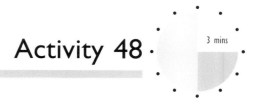

Activity 48 · 3 mins

Why might it be a drawback that the descriptions are derived from the webpage itself?

_____

_____

_____

The answer to this Activity can be found on page 124.

Search engines are fairly indiscriminate. Some of the results they give may come from reputable sources and provide you with valuable up-to-date information, but others may be out of date, inaccurate or incomplete.

With a 'first generation' search engine such as the original **AltaVista** (www.altavista.com) the results of a search are usually presented in 'term ranked' order. This means that a document appears higher in the list of results if your search terms occur very frequently in the document, or in the document title, or near the beginning of the document, or close together in the document.

Many, if not all, first generation search engines have transformed themselves into portals and/or have some 'second-generation' features, because basic term-ranked searching is indiscriminate and gives far too many results.

'Second generation' search engines such as **Google** (www.google.com) order search results by links or popularity, by concept, by keyword, or by type of site. These search engines generally give better quality results because there is at least some human element in determining what is relevant.

For example, one of the ways that Google ranks pages is according to the number of other pages that link to it. The more Web authors who have decided that it is worth including a link to a page, the more likely it is that the page is useful and relevant to the topic you are searching for.

Teoma (www.teoma.com) organizes its results into three sections: pages listed in link-ranked order; a list of suggestions to refine and narrow your search; and a list of resources such as collections of relevant links written by experts and enthusiasts.

The link ranking is slightly different to Google's. A site is ranked based on 'subject-specific popularity', in other words the number of same-subject pages that reference it, not just general popularity.

Teoma is also behind the popular **AskJeeves** search engine, but you may find that Teoma gives better results for business research purposes.

Ixquick (www.ixquick.com/) is a **metasearch engine**, which means that it uses multiple other search engines simultaneously and returns the results in a single list with duplicate files removed.

Ixquick only returns the top ten results from the source search services, so in theory you can harness the collective judgement of many search tools about the relevancy and usefulness of sites on a topic all in a single search.

By default the sources Ixquick uses are country specific. In other words it checks where you are dialling in from (the UK, say, as opposed to the USA) and then uses search tools that mainly return results from that country. You can of course override this if you wish to look at French sites or Danish sites, etc.

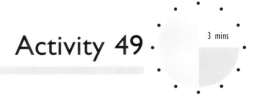

Activity 49 · 3 mins

Why might country-specific searching be a drawback to a search?

The answer to this Activity can be found on page 124.

3.5 Internet databases (the 'deep Web')

Many websites consist of pages that are generated 'dynamically' using content stored in a database. In other words the contents that you see are only assembled—and put into a Web page that your browser can read—on request. The page does not actually exist in the form of a saved file and therefore it can't be found by a search engine or listed in a directory.

Typical sites that use databases will be those that have frequently changing data such as airline information sites, and particularly news-related sites with up to the minute current stories and archived stories and articles material perhaps going back several years.

Such content is called the 'invisible' Web or the 'deep' Web and estimates suggest that there is now at least 500 times more material in this form than there is on the conventional Web. The reason is because it is more efficient to store data in this way. Most pages consist mainly of standard elements like logos and navigation menus and tables defining layout, so it is more efficient to create a single template for all the elements that do not change and simply 'plug' the required information into a space in the template.

Clearly you cannot afford to ignore such a large source of information, but how do you find it? The only way you can do so is to search the database itself. This is not as complicated as it sounds: from the point of view of the user you either just click on what appears to be an ordinary link or you type a few words in the 'Search' box on the site itself.

For example if you were using http://www.dictionary.com and wanted to find definitions for the term 'dynamic' you would simply type 'dynamic' into the search box and click on the 'Look it up' button. This takes you to the URL http://dictionary.reference.com/search?q=dynamic: the part of the URL after the question mark is actually an instruction to extract relevant material from the site's database about the term 'dynamic' and present it in a Web page.

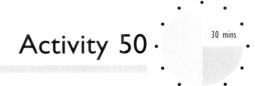

Activity 50 · 30 mins

S/NVQ D1.1

This Activity may provide the basis of appropriate evidence for your S/NVQ portfolio. If you are intending to take this course of action, you may wish to print off copies of pages you visit as evidence that you have attempted the task.

Pick two or three topics that are relevant to the work and industry sector of your organization.

Log onto the Internet and try a search on that topic using each of the search tools referred to in the previous pages in turn (Yahoo, Google, etc.).

Which search tool gives you the most satisfactory results?

You may also wish to see if you can find portals or vortals specific to your business. Also, see if you can find a news-related site that has database content. This is not necessarily easy because there is no easy way of knowing but, as a hint, database-driven pages will usually have an extension such as .cgi, .asp, .php, .jsp, or .cfm instead of the usual .htm, and when you click on links the URL will have a string like this attached to it:

?articleID=164888&fromsearch=true&keywords=your%20topic

4 Refining a search

Many people—especially new users—find searching the Web extremely frustrating because they cannot find what they are looking for quickly enough. In this section we describe some of the things you can do to make your searches more productive.

4.1 Use your initial search proactively

If you are researching a new topic the chances are that you will not be very familiar with the concepts and terminology of that subject.

In this case, when you do an initial search spend a few moments skim reading the first few results pages. They probably won't tell you what you want to know, but they may well include words and phrases that you could add to your search terms to give more useful results, or words and phrases that you could exclude from your search (we'll explain how to do this in a moment).

Some search engines display words such as More Like This or Similar pages next to each entry. For instance if you searched for 'management tips' you would find that one of the first few results was to do with time management. If time management happened to be your specific interest you could get a new list of sites specifically on that subject simply by clicking on the Similar Pages or More Like This link.

4.2 Restrict the search area

Some search engines have options to restrict the number of sites searched, for instance to UK sites only, or to English language sites only. Even if that option is not available you will generally find that if you simply add UK to your search term the results will be closer to the ones you need.

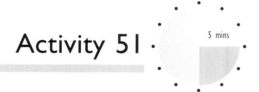

Activity 51

Suppose you were searching for a stationery supplier. Using your favourite search engine try a search for 'office supplies' and make a mental note of the first few results. Then try adding UK to the search term and see if the results improve (in the sense that you get links to the websites of suppliers you might actually purchase from, as opposed to suppliers in California). Then search for 'office supplies' and add the name of your nearest large town.

Finally, jot down any other ways you can think of to refine this search.

_____

_____

_____

_____

4.3 Advanced search techniques

On many (though not all) sites the search facility allows you to use **symbols** and/or what are known as **Boolean operators** to help refine what should and should not be searched for. These so-called 'advanced' searching techniques aren't actually particularly advanced, and they are extremely useful.

Different search engines have slightly different rules for formulating queries, so it is always a good idea to **read the help files** at the site before you start a search.

Plus signs (+)

If you put a plus sign (+) directly in front of a word (with no space) this tells the search engine that the word **must** be present in all the pages that are found. So if you type **+management +tips**, you will only get pages that contain both words (though not necessarily together or in the order you specify).

Minus signs (–)

As you might expect, the – sign works in the opposite way to +. If you put a minus sign directly in front of a word the search engine will **ignore** any documents that contain that word. So, if you type **+management +tips –racing** you will avoid pages that have tips on the horses!

However intuitive you are at using the minus sign you are still likely to get links that you are not interested in. You probably would not think of typing, say, **+management +tips –pest**, for example, because the idea of pest management in gardening would probably (or hopefully, at least) not occur to you when you were thinking about managing your workteam.

Quotation marks (")

To find **only** pages that contain the phrase **management tips**, with the words together in that order, you enclose them in double quotation marks: **"management tips"**. This is very useful so long as your phrase is only two or three words long or if you know exactly how the phrase should be worded (because it is a famous quotation, say).

OR

There is a good chance that some of the pages relevant to your search will use alternative words to the ones you first think of. If you can guess what the alternatives might be you can use OR to make the search engine look for pages that contain at least one of them: for instance **management +tips OR hints OR advice**.

Activity 52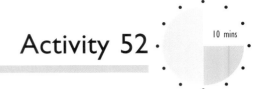

10 mins

User-friendly advanced searching

Increasingly sites are recognizing that people want more than a basic search facility, and include an option to do an 'Advanced' search via an on-screen form. This has much the same effect as using Boolean operators, but you may find it easier to understand and easier to construct your queries.

An example of an advanced search page is shown in the illustration below.

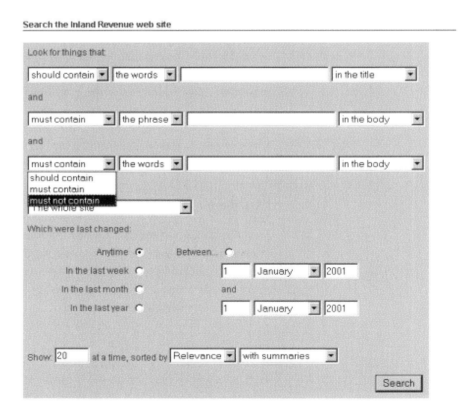

©Crown Copyright 2002

5 Evaluating Internet information

Anyone with Internet access can publish anything they like on the Internet. Some sites are created by people with expert knowledge while others are completely amateur. Some are updated daily or hourly or even minute by minute, while others are hopelessly out of date.

If you do a search for cancer research, say, one of the pages you are directed to may be a page of tasteless jokes, while others may appear to be reputable but may actually be written by people with no medical knowledge or training at all. As with any information resource, therefore, it is important to evaluate what you find on the Internet.

All of what we said in Session A about valid information applies equally to information that you find on the Web. You may wish to turn back to Session A and remind yourself of the key points. Here are a few additional things to look out for.

- You should be able to find out about the background of the creators of the site. Most sites have an 'About us' link directly available from the home page, and this page may give you details of the qualifications and expertise of the authors, how well established the organization is, and so on.
- Look for evidence of the date of the material: this will often be given at the foot of the page.
- Even the address gives you some indication of the likely authoritativeness of the site. You can often spot an amateur page because it will have something like '~suesmith' in the address. This indicates that it is an individual's site on free Web space provided by an ISP such as Virgin, AOL, FreeServe, and so on. It may still be a very good and useful page, but it will not have any 'official' status.
- Don't take the information presented at face value. For example one of the results from your search on 'cancer research' may be a set of pages written by animal rights activists. That's fine if that is what you are looking for, and the information may be perfectly accurate, but bear in mind that the material will be biased towards a particular point of view.

6 Intranets

Let's not forget that your own organization may be a valuable source of information on various topics, especially if it is a large one.

The topic of retrieving information from corporate databases is covered in more detail in another workbook in this series: *Storing and Retrieving Information*.

Most companies have networked systems which may give you access to a variety of databases containing customer and supplier information, product and service information, information about your staff, and so on.

Many organizations have also set up an 'intranet', which is the term used for an organization's own mini version of the Internet, using the organization's own servers and networked computers combined with Internet technology.

Intranets are used for a wide variety of purposes such as newsletters, training material, procedure and policy manuals, and directories of websites that are particularly relevant to the organization's business.

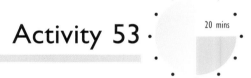

Activity 53 · 20 mins

S/NVQ D1.1, D1.2

This Activity may provide the basis of appropriate evidence for your S/NVQ portfolio. If you are intending to take this course of action, it might be better to print off relevant pages and/or write your answers on separate sheets of paper.

Does your organization have an intranet?

- If so, find or create a summary of its contents suitable as a guide for a new recruit. Is there any information not currently included that you think should be added? Make a note of such items and find out from your IT department what you have to do to get this new content added.
- If not, create a similar summary listing the contents that you think it would be useful to put onto an intranet. If you are feeling very adventurous you may wish to discuss this with your IT department and see if you can set up an intranet, even if it is only for use by your own workteam.

7 Internet abuse

Leaving aside e-mail problems, there are two main types of Internet abuse that you may come up against.

Personal use during working hours

The Internet can be used for all sorts of personal activities such as booking holidays, managing a bank account or simply pursuing leisure interests. This is a waste of working time and may involve other telecom and ISP costs if the organization does not have a permanent Internet connection.

On the other hand, there is evidence that some employers actively encourage their staff to use the Internet for leisure purposes, though there may often be a policy such as only allowing access for personal use during lunch hours.

Downloading inappropriate material

Inappropriate material means pornography in particular, but also includes computer games, illegal software, and so on. Aside from wasting time this may offend other employees, endanger the organization's computers, or even implicate the organization in a criminal act. The individual who illegally downloads material from the Internet may be personally liable to criminal prosecution as well as being in breach of their contract of employment. You should make sure that your team are aware of these risks and you should never turn a blind eye if you think that anyone is viewing or downloading such material.

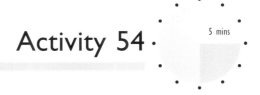

Activity 54

5 mins

You suspect that members of your workteam are abusing the privilege of Internet access. What actions could you take?

_____

_____

_____

_____

A study in October 2002 indicated that two-thirds of UK employers undertake some monitoring of their employees' use of the Internet, although in most cases this simply means that they keep an eye on how much time is spent. These are the actions we would suggest.

- In the first place you should remind all staff of the organization's policies with regard to Internet use. If there is no policy you should draft one, probably in consultation with your own manager.
- In principle you may well be able to view a log of all sites visited by each employee (networking software will usually record this information). However, this is not recommended in the Information Commissioner's draft code of practice on 'The use of personal data in employer/employee relationships' except in exceptional circumstances.
- In any case very close monitoring is impractical: it would most probably take up a great deal of your time, and you cannot always tell whether a site is 'inappropriate' simply from its name (you may have to look at the suspicious material yourself!).
- A much better approach is to use a software solution. It is possible to restrict Internet access so that people cannot visit certain kinds of site. You can also restrict the times of day that Internet access is available.

Self-assessment 3

10 mins

1   Another name for the Internet is the 'World Wide Web'. True or False?

2   What are the main differences between directories and search engines?

3   What is the deep Web?

4   How could you make sure that a specific phrase appeared on the Web pages in your search results?

5   What should be the key points in an organization's policy regarding staff use of the Internet?

Answers to these questions can be found on page 121.

8 Summary

- Connection to the Internet is usually made via an Internet Service Provider, though you may not be aware of this if you access the Internet via a work computer.

- Most people use the Internet through interface programs called browsers such as Microsoft Internet Explorer. Browsers make Web surfing more user-friendly.

- Sites are navigated via clickable menus and links. There is no standard format, but a good navigation system is one of the main indicators of a well-designed and useful site.

- Web content consists not only of standard Web (.htm) pages but also material in other formats such as Flash animations and pdf files.

- Often you will know the precise address of a website. Sometimes you will come across a useful one as a result of fairly random browsing.

- Search tools fall into three categories although the lines between them are fairly blurred.

- Directories offer links to Web pages that have been evaluated by human beings and are organized into subject categories.

- Search engines retrieve links to, and brief descriptions of, websites containing a word or phrase entered by the user. Little or no human judgement is involved, although some search engines give more prominence to sites that many other sites have links to.

- The deep Web or invisible Web is Web content that cannot be found by a search engine because it is stored in a database. These can only be searched by visiting the site itself and using the site's own search facilities.

- There are several ways of refining a search to get more useful results. Many search engines include a link such as 'More like this' or 'Similar pages'. Most allow you to use symbols such as + and − and inverted commas to specify what content should and should not be included. Some sites have their own 'advanced' search tools where you simply enter your search criteria into an onscreen form.

- Evaluating Internet information is similar to evaluating any other kind of information. There may be certain clues on a website such as the 'About us' link, the date and the form of the address.

- Many organizations have an 'intranet' (a mini version of the Internet for internal use) for information such as newsletters, training materials and procedures manuals.

- There are two main types of Internet abuse: personal use for non work-related purposes and downloading inappropriate material. Prevention is better than cure: it is possible to restrict the amount of time people spend online and bar particular types of sites by technological means.

Performance checks

1 Quick quiz

Write down your answer in the space below to the following questions on *Collecting Information*.

Question 1   Information is data (text and figures) that has been processed in some way. What do we mean by 'processed'?

_____

_____

Question 2   Draw a diagram in the space below showing the cycle of business activity.

Question 3   What is the mnemonic for the qualities of good information and what do the letters stand for?

_____

_____

_____

_____

_____

_____

_____

_____

Question 4   List five sources of internal business information

_____

_____

_____

_____

_____

_____

Question 5   There are two main reasons why information may not be valid. What are they?

_____

_____

_____

Question 6   Which of the items of information below would be difficult or impossible to collect using technological devices?

A   Shoppers' preferred route around supermarket aisles
B   Your workteam's sense of job satisfaction
C   Number of telephone complaints received about a product
D   Unusual noises made by a car engine

_____

_____

Question 7   Identify and explain two types of open question designed to encourage people to explain what they mean in more detail.

_____

_____

_____

_____

Question 8   A draft questionnaire by a food manufacturer includes the question: 'How much did you enjoy eating this product?'

What is wrong with the question and how could it be redesigned?

_____

_____

_____

_____

_____

_____

Question 9   Why might you sometimes be prevented from collecting information?

_____

_____

_____

_____

_____

Question 10   Which is the best option for getting an overview of the entire contents of a website?

A   A Web directory such as Yahoo!
B   A site map
C   Text links at the foot of the home page
D   The More Like This link in a search engine

Question 11 What is a metasearch engine and why might it give better results than a simpler search tool?

_____
_____
_____
_____

Question 12 Why might you use the term OR in an Internet search.

_____
_____
_____

Question 13 You are evaluating the validity of information found in the Internet that criticizes a new government policy on corporation tax. What seven questions should you ask?

_____
_____
_____
_____
_____
_____
_____
_____
_____

Question 14 To connect to a database on another computer within an organization it is necessary to use an intranet.

True or False? Explain your answer.

_____
_____
_____

Question 15 It is illegal under the Data Protection Act 1998 for an employer to collect and store data about an employee's sexual preferences when downloading pornography at work.

True or False? Explain your answer.

_____
_____
_____

Answers to these questions can be found on pages 125–127.

60 mins

2 Workbook assessment

Read the following case study and then deal with the questions that follow, writing your answers on a separate sheet of paper.

Dean plc is a manufacturer of components for the European consumer electronics industry. They make items such as audio jack plugs and sockets, plastic knobs and slider controls and cabinet corners, and other plastic parts.

The company employs 50 administrative staff and nearly 300 people in the factory or in production-related roles. You work in the customer service department and deal with audio connector sales.

- Spend up to ten minutes gathering as much information as you can about audio connectors, using appropriate valid sources. Bear in mind any constraints on collection of information.
- Imagine that a new customer has phoned up and is being very vague about their requirements. Script the questions that you might ask over the telephone to help the customer explain their needs more clearly.
- Draw up a list of items of *internal* information that you may need to help with day-to-day management of your workteam. Beside each item note down the source and the technical or other means by which the information would be collected.
- Draw up a list and brief descriptions of ten websites that production managers at Deal plc might find useful when planning for the future. (Don't include general search engines and the like, but you may wish to consider government sites and European sites, if appropriate.)

3 Work-based assignment

60 mins

S/NVQ D1.1, D1.2

The time guide for this assignment gives you an approximate idea of how long it is likely to take you to write up your findings. You will find you need to spend some additional time gathering information, perhaps talking to colleagues and thinking about the assignment.

The results of your efforts should be presented on separate sheets of paper.

If you prefer you could prepare a Web page (for instance using Microsoft Word or Excel and the Save As Web Page option) for possible use on your organization's intranet. We do not expect you to be able to program it for 'live' use.

This assignment is designed to help you develop Personal Competence in:

- communicating;
- searching for information.

Your response to this assignment could provide appropriate evidence for your S/NVQ portfolio for element D1.1 Gather required information, and, if the results are used to inform others, D1.2 Inform and advise others.

In Session B we posed the following scenario:

Suppose you are in charge of Workteam A and you provide a service to Workteam B. You want to find out whether there is any more you and your team can do to satisfy the needs of the other team.

One of our suggestions was that you discussed the issues with the fictional manager of Workteam B and then prepared a questionnaire for the members of the other workteam.

We are now going to ask you to carry out a similar exercise within your own organization.

- Identify the 'internal customers' for the work that your workteam does: these will be other departments or workteams who are affected by your work.
- Establish by discussion with relevant colleagues what is their understanding of the work done by your workteam and what they expect of you.
- Draw up a questionnaire that aims to discover how satisfied your internal customers are with the work of your team and whether there is anything more you and your team can do to satisfy customer needs.
- Pilot test the questionnaire and rewrite the questions as necessary based on the whether the responses give you the information you needed.

Reflect and review

1 Reflect and review

Now that you have completed your work on *Collecting Information*, let us review the objectives that we set at the beginning.

Our first objective was:

■ understand the need for information and gather information relevant to your own area of responsibility

If you think about it you will quickly realize that it is impossible to get anything done at all unless you have information of some kind, even if it is simply information that you know by experience.

Hopefully you have now conducted a thorough review of the information you need to do your job. Perhaps you have identified some areas where you don't currently have enough information; perhaps some of the information that is reported to you regularly is not used or not needed.

■ Make a note of any changes you intend to make regarding your own information needs at work.

_____

_____

The next objective was:

■ identify a range of information sources which may be used in the organization

We discussed a very wide range of external information sources, and we pointed out that it is often quicker to have a few good reference books beside you than to use the Internet on every occasion.

■ Are you comfortable using reference books and are you happy that you get the best out of the ones that are most useful to you in your job? This is usually a matter of taking the trouble to read the introduction, and understanding what symbols or typographical conventions are used and how things are arranged.

■ Make a note of any extra effort you intend to make in this connection.

Your own organization, of course, will be a major source of information for day-to-day management of activities. It is quite possible that other people outside your team have information that would be useful to you, not because they are keeping it from you (or not normally!), but simply because they don't realize you need it.

■ Have you made sure that all the members of your team understand your organization's systems well enough to be able to get the information they need? More training may be required, or a clearer system.

■ Are you sure that you are fully aware of the information resources your organization has to offer? It may be worthwhile chatting about this to managers in other departments that you deal with.

■ Note down the actions you will need to take to improve your use of internal information.

The next objective was to:

■ identify means of collecting and recording data and/or information

Automatic collection of data is going on all around you and the number of devices available to assist with data collection is increasing all the time. Whenever you can collect information that you need in a painless way by using technology it is worth setting up the appropriate system, if it is not too expensive, because the time saved can be much better used. You should also think about how your information will be stored and analysed, for example using databases and spreadsheets, because this may affect the method of collection.

■ Have you identified any information-gathering activities that you currently do manually that could be automated?

- Do you use databases and spreadsheets for storing and analysing your information?

- Make a note of any information-gathering activities that could be automated here and what extra resources you will need (new software, new hardware, and so on).

- Investigate whether databases and spreadsheets are used in your organization. Could it benefit from using them or from taking more advantage of what they offer?

Nevertheless, a great deal of information that may be useful can't easily be collected by automatic devices, especially when it involves attitudes, desires and feelings. Besides that, it is a pleasure to talk to real live human beings!

We described a number of techniques that you can use to get the information you require from people in conversation – partly by thinking more carefully about how you ask questions, and partly by encouraging you to listen more carefully to the answers.

- How effective do you think you are at finding out what you need to know in conversation (from your team members, from your own manager, from customers, and so on)? Is there anything you can do to improve? Make a plan here.

The next objective was:

■ recognize any constraints on the collection of, and access to, data

Hopefully you now think about copyright issues before you photocopy vast sections of published material or download material from the Internet. In most cases you will simply be doing your own research to find out more about a topic, but if there is any possibility that you will publish the material and give others the impression that it is your own then great care is needed. Just think how you would feel if you spent ages preparing a report for your manager and then your team members copied it and claimed it was theirs!

If you deal with the general public you need to be aware of the rights of individuals regarding 'personal data'. The same is true of your fellow employees' rights, particularly where 'sensitive' data is concerned.

The next objective was:

- check sources and validity of data

  Although there is a huge amount of information available, and it is more accessible than ever, a great deal of it is not good information, and some of it is not valid information. You should be assessing validity whenever you come across a potential new source: you should be thinking about whether it is up to date, whether the writer is an expert, whether there are any signs of bias and so on.

  - Are you satisfied that all your sources of information (whether internal or external) are providing you with good, valid information? Do you always bother to check? If not, have you identified better sources and resolved to develop better, more careful habits?

  - What sorts of thing could go wrong if you or your team members don't bother to check the validity of information that you use? Try to think of three or four examples: that will hopefully be enough to scare you into being more diligent!

The final objective – although you may already have included it in some of your answers and plans above – referred to the Internet.

- use the Internet as an information resource

  You have probably used the Internet at least for leisure purposes. You may formerly have been one of the many people who complains that it is impossible to find what you want: it is one of the most often cited reasons for not using the Internet.

  Hopefully this book has given you some hints and shown you some tools that will help you to improve your Web searching so that you find better results more quickly.

- What is your preferred search tool for information related to your business?

_____

- Have you found any new resources that you will use in future: a useful portal for your type of business, say, or a way of doing advanced searches that take you exactly where you want to go? Make a note of any great new discoveries here.

_____

_____

_____

_____

2 Action plan

Use this plan to further develop for yourself a course of action you want to take. Make a note in the left-hand column of the issues or problems you want to tackle, and then decide what you intend to do, and make a note in column 2.

The resources you need might include time, materials, information or money. You may need to negotiate for some of them, but they could be something easily acquired, like half an hour of somebody's time, or a chapter of a book. Put whatever you need in column 3. No plan means anything without a timescale, so put a realistic target completion date in column 4.

Finally, describe the outcome you want to achieve as a result of this plan, whether it is for your own benefit or advancement, or a more efficient way of doing things.

Desired outcomes			
1 Issues	2 Action	3 Resources	4 Target completion
Actual outcomes			

3 Extensions

Extension 1

Book	*Management Research: An Introduction*
Author	Mark Easterby-Smith, Richard Thorpe
Edition	2001
Publisher	Sage Publications Ltd
ISBN	0761972854

Extension 2

Data collection devices – the latest developments

Major monthly computer magazines such as *PC World*, *MacUser*, and so on. Study both articles and advertisements to keep track of falling prices and the ever-growing range of options.

Extension 3

Book	*Questionnaire Design*
Author	Alan V. Oppenheim
Edition	2000
Publisher	Continuum International Publishing Group
ISBN	0826451764

Extension 4

Data Protection Act 1998

Extensive information and guidance (including a link to the full text of the Act, how to register, and so on) is available at the website of the office of the Information Commissioner.

http://www.dataprotection.gov.uk/

Extension 5

Book	*Understanding Copyright*
Author	Graham Cornish
Edition	2000
Publisher	Hodder & Stoughton
ISBN	0340782412

Extension 6

Book	*The Internet Research Handbook: An Introductory Guide for the Social Sciences*
Author	Niall O'Dochartaigh
Edition	2001
Publisher	Sage Publications Ltd
ISBN	0761964401

Extension 7   *Websites*

Many website addresses are given in the appropriate place in this book.

If you have no idea where to start, a very good choice is the **BBC** site: http://www.bbc.co.uk.

You may also wish to look at the website of your favourite broadsheet **newspaper**. These require you to register before you can view detailed content, but (at the time of publication of this book) registration is free.

Financial Times: http://www.ft.com/
The Times: http://www.timesonline.co.uk/
The Telegraph: http://www.telegraph.co.uk/
The Independent: http://www.independent.co.uk/
The Guardian: http://www.guardian.co.uk/

You may also find that the **trade magazines** relevant to your business have websites, though you will probably need to subscribe to the magazine to get full access.

4 Answers to self-assessment questions

**Self-assessment 1
on page 32**

1   Organizations record transactions primarily because they are legally obliged to do so, but the information is also used in the management of the business. Information about previous transactions is used as the raw material for planning and decision-making. Information about current transactions is the raw material for control and performance measurement.

2   ■ Authority means that the source of the information should be as reliable as possible.
    ■ Clarity means that the information should be communicated using an appropriate channel, and it should be presented clearly.
    ■ Economy means that the benefits obtained from the information must be greater than the costs of collecting and analysing it.

3   No. Information can be valid in the sense that it is accurate and it comes from a reliable source. But this does not necessarily mean that it possesses any of the other qualities of good information: it may not be timely or user-targeted, for instance; it may not even be relevant.

4　A primary source of information is as close as you can get to the origin, for example an original document such as a birth certificate. A secondary source is information reported by a third party, for instance a biography telling you the birth date of a famous person.

5　Types of specialist information provider include:

- advice or information bureaux, such as a tourist information office;
- news agencies such as Reuters;
- consultancies and research organizations providing information on specific industries or conducting marketing research;
- subscription-based organizations such as the Institute of Directors;
- professional bodies such as the Law Society.

6　Types of computer validation check include:

- a **format** check which makes sure that data entered is in the correct format, for instance the right number of digits or the right combination of letters and numbers in the right order;
- a **range** check which makes sure that information lies within pre-determined limits;
- a **limit** check makes sure that information does not lie beyond predetermined limits;
- a **calculation** check which applies pre-determined rules to make sure that numbers have the correct mathematical relationship.

7　Ways of double-checking the source of information include:

- checking against what you know for certain;
- checking against what you judge to be reasonable;
- checking against what you can easily find out, for instance against internal documents;
- checking by conducting further external research.

Self-assessment 2 on page 80–81

1　Three types of information you might need when allocating work are:

- who is available to work;
- what their skills are;
- what work needs to be done and how long it will take.

2　Self-reporting is performance monitoring carried out by the person who actually does the work (for example time sheets or job sheets), as opposed to a system that measures work in a controlled way such as a clocking in system or computer log.

3　A computer might record logging-in and logging-out times, the number of transactions processed and how long each one took, and the number of errors or revisions. You may have thought of further examples.

4 Types of computer-linked data collection devices include:

- keyboard and mouse;
- communications links;
- scratch pads;
- key pads;
- credit card and smart card readers;
- bar-code readers;
- document scanners;
- graphics tablets;
- touch-sensitive screens;
- hand-held terminals;
- voice recognition systems.

5 A field is an individual piece of information in a database record.

6 You can use Filter to display only those records that fulfil the criteria you set for one column.

7 Closed questions give people a choice of predetermined answers or can simply be answered with a 'Yes' or 'No, a tick in a box or a very short factual answer. Open questions let people respond at greater length in their own words.

8 When listening to an answer you should try to detect:

- what the person wants to say;
- what the person is trying not to say;
- what the person is saying, but doesn't mean, or is lying about;
- what the person is having difficulty saying.

9 Things to avoid when designing questionnaires are:

- avoid open questions as far as possible;
- avoid calculations;
- explain and give instructions;
- assure anonymity or ask permission to retain details;
- say thank you and/or offer incentives;
- make sure that the questions will provide all the information you require.

10 Observation is a suitable method for collection information when:

- the activity or behaviour is visible: feelings, beliefs and attitudes can't be accurately judged simply by observation;
- the activity or behaviour is something that is done frequently or repeatedly and only takes a short time.

11   Types of sensitive information under the Data Protection Act 1988 include:

- racial or ethnic origin;
- political opinions;
- religious beliefs;
- trade union membership;
- physical or mental health or condition;
- information about sexual life;
- offences committed or allegedly committed;
- details of court proceedings or sentences.

12   This is false. Copyright covers the way the words or notes or visual images are arranged, not the idea they convey: it protects the **form** or **expression** of an idea, not the idea itself.

Self-assessment 3 on page 103

1   False. The World Wide Web is just the part of the Internet that is usually accessed using a browser. The Internet also includes e-mail, where information is exchanged using the simple mail transfer protocol (smtp), file transfer protocol (ftp), most often used for uploading files to a website, and other services.

2   A directory is organized into categories and only lists pages that have been evaluated by a human being. A search engine lists pages according to criteria such as how often a search term appears in a page or how many other pages link to it. In practice most directories now have some of the features of directories and vice versa.

3   The deep Web is a term used to describe Internet content that is held in databases (rather than in conventional HTML files) and only assembled into a viewable web page on request. The deep web is estimated to have at least 500 times more content than is available in conventional web pages.

4   To ensure that a specific phrase appears in pages in the search results the phrase should be enclosed in double inverted commas. If you said 'put a plus sign in front of it' that is only partially right, because that would only ensure that the first word of the phrase was included.

5   The policy should cover the following points.

- Whether staff are permitted to access the Internet for personal use and if so for how long and at what times.
- The downloading of inappropriate material should be prohibited.
- Care should be taken to avoid breaching copyright.
- The policy should explain what disciplinary action will be taken in a case of Internet abuse.

Reflect and review

5 Answers to activities

Activity 6
on page 11

UK Post Code Format								
Position	1	2	(3)	(4)	5	6	7	8
Format	A	A or N	(A or N)	(A or N)	Space	N	A	A
Disallowed		I, Z						C, I, K, M, O
A = any letter except those disallowed. N = number (0–9)								
Minimum length: 6 characters. Brackets: characters may be omitted at positions 3 and 4.								
Samples: W1 3PV, E2C 4AB, LS3 8QX, CV17 3LT. Sole exception: GIR 0AA								

Activity 15
on page 28

Checking against what you know or what you think is true has the danger that you might be wrong, while checking against an internal source has the danger that the internal source might be wrong. Hopefully this won't be the case very often, but you should beware of getting complacent, even if you do seem to be right a lot of the time.

Activity 32
on page 55

Fields required:
- Title
- First name
- Last name
- Address 1
- Address 2
- City
- PostCode
- Date
- Date of last service
- Service date

You may have chosen slightly different codes, and given them different names, but this set of codes works with the letter below. The proposed service date would be entered onto the database by an administrator, and altered if the customer called to rearrange.

122

The codes in this letter are produced in MicroSoft Word.

Boilers Ltd
50 Gas Works Rd
Yourtown
Tel: 03945 679320

«Title»«FirstName»«LastName»
«Address1»
«Address2»
«City»
«PostCode»

«Date»

Dear «Title»«LastName»

We note from our records that you last had your boiler serviced on «dateoflastservice». We have booked in your annual service for «Servicedate». Please call us to rearrange if this is not convenient.

We are sure you are well aware of the benefits of regular servicing for gas boilers and we look forward to making sure your boiler remains in good working order for the coming year.

Yours sincerely

G White
Chief Service Engineer

Activity 36 on page 62

Answer 1 contains far too much information. Answer 2 gives an exotic name that is probably something chosen by the paint manufacturer, so unless you happen to be familiar with sea thistles it doesn't give you any useful information at all. It would probably have been far better to give a list of choices in the question: red, blue, green, etc.

Activity 37 on page 63

Here are some suggestions. Your answers will probably be different, but make sure your questions cannot be answered by a very short answer.

- What would you like to accompany that?
- Describe what you like and dislike about your job.
- Tell me about how you are going to spend your weekend.

Activity 39 on page 70

The answer could be considered to fall under the category 'face-to-face'. However, if similar answers occur very frequently it may be worth creating a separate category such as 'Gestures' in your analysis.

Activity 40 on page 71

This question gives no indication of what format to use for the date and this will make the results more difficult to analyse because some people will write the number of the month while others will write the name (probably abbreviated in various different ways); some people will use four digits for the year, others will use two.

Here is a better version. Alternatively you could spell it out in the question: 'For 3rd April 2004 write 03–04–2004'.

```
                          D   D      M   M       Y   Y   Y   Y
                        ┌───┬───┬───┬───┬───┬───┬───┬───┬───┬───┐
Date of purchase        │   │   │ – │   │   │ – │   │   │   │   │
                        └───┴───┴───┴───┴───┴───┴───┴───┴───┴───┘
```

**Activity 41
on page 70**

If you just ignore the comments this may make you appear arrogant or uncaring, but if you confront the person who was critical you will undermine the promise of anonymity for the whole workteam.

Possibly the best approach would be to issue a message to all the members of the team inviting anybody who wanted to discuss the issues further to a one-to-one meeting. There is a pretty good chance that your critic knew that their handwriting would be recognized and may welcome the opportunity.

However, there is no 'correct' answer to this question. It would depend very much on your relationship with your team and with the individual in question, what the criticisms were, whether they were valid, and possibly a host of other issues.

**Activity 43
on page 78**

A computer program is actually just a collection of 'words' and symbols from a computer language, arranged in a certain way devised by the programmer. (Or more strictly it is a collection of words and symbols arranged in a certain way and then translated into the 1s and 0s of computer code.) In this sense it is very similar to a novel or a poem or a piece of music.

**Activity 48
on page 92**

If the description is written by the webpage author you have no guarantee that it is an accurate description. The description might say 'This is the most popular webpage in the world on subject X', but that need not be true!

**Activity 49
on page 93**

It is not a drawback if you are looking for a local supplier, say, or for a job within reasonable travelling distance of your home. But if it is pure information that you are after and the search only considers UK-based sites you may well miss some much better information from authors elsewhere in the world.

6 ■ Answers to the quick quiz

Answer 1   Processing typically involves: categorising and sorting the data under meaningful headings; calculating totals, sub-totals, percentages and so on; and summarising and drawing conclusions.

Answer 2

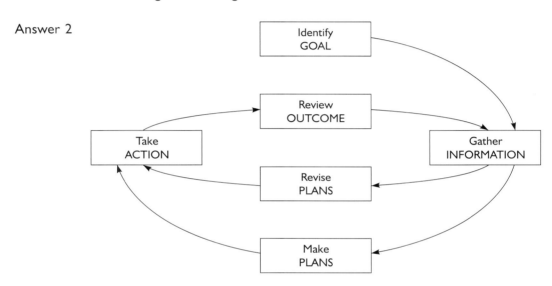

Answer 3   The mnemonic is A.C.C.U.R.A.T.E. which stands for:

A   Accurate
C   Complete
C   Clear
U   User-targeted
R   Relevant
A   Authoritative
T   Timely
E   Economic

Answer 4   There are many examples. We've put them into general categories but you may have been more specific:

■ information sent out to others, such as letters, invoices, statements, brochures, price lists, promotional material, orders, cheques;
■ formal information flowing around the organization such as e-mails, memos, notices on notice boards, minutes of meetings, internal reports, business plans;

- information required to operate internal systems such as job cards, timesheets, clocking-in systems, stock requisitions and the accounting system as a whole;
- rule books, operational manuals, technical drawings, procedural guidelines, lists of approved suppliers, policy documents, and reports on incidents, disputes and other issues that have arisen in the past;
- personnel records;
- informal communications between managers and their workteams.

Answer 5   Reasons for information not being valid are:

- if it was not recorded correctly;
- if you used an unreliable source.

Answer 6   The best answer is b. Shoppers routes could be recorded by cameras or by tracking devices in shopping trolleys and baskets. Complaints could be measured via the phone system (the number of calls put through to the complaints department). You could simply tape record the car engine, although there are many sophisticated diagnostic tools available to the car maintenance and servicing industry.

Answer 7   A probing question asks someone to explain something they have said in more detail. Problem-solving questions put a person in a particular situation and ask them how they would deal with it. The Friendly Martian technique asks people to explain something on the assumption that the person they are talking to has no prior knowledge.

Answer 8   The problem with the question is that it could elicit too large a variety of responses for useful analysis. It would be better to give people a scale.

Please rate your enjoyment of this product on a scale of 1 to 5, where 1 is 'Did not enjoy at all' and 5 is 'Enjoyed very much'.
1
2
3
4
5

Answer 9   Reasons for not collecting information include the following.

- Sometimes the cost of collecting it will outweigh the benefits.
- Sometimes people will just refuse to tell you what you want to know.
- Sometimes people may be unwilling to give you information unless you pay them for it.
- Some information is subject to the Official Secrets Act or commercial restrictions and you will not be allowed to look at it.
- Some information is 'personal' and you cannot store and re-use it without asking the permission of the individual in question.

- Much information is protected by copyright and you cannot store and re-use it without asking the permission of the copyright owner.

Answer 10   A site map (option b) is the best option, if there is one or, failing that, text links at the foot of the page, if they are present. Directories and search engines do not necessarily list all the contents and may be out-of-date.

Answer 11   A metasearch engine is one that uses multiple other search engines simultaneously and returns the results in a single list with duplicate files removed. In theory this means that you can harness the collective judgement of many search tools all within a single search.

Answer 12   OR can be used when you suspect that some of the pages relevant to your search will use alternative words to the ones you first think of, for instance: 'business OR management +research'; 'office +machines OR equipment OR supplies'.

Answer 13   If you mentioned the date on the webpage lose a mark: we told you that it was a **new** government policy so comment on it will not be out of date! Your best source of information to answer this question is Session A, where you would find the following checklist against most of which you could judge the 'About us' page on the site.

- Is the source experienced in this field?
- Does the source understand the issues?
- Does the source have access to up-to-date information?
- Has the source consulted other appropriate sources?
- Is the source free of personal biases about the matter?
- Does the source have a good track record for giving reliable opinions?
- Is the opinion consistent with other information available?

Answer 14   False. Strictly speaking an intranet uses Internet protocols, such as http, and a web server. This is not necessary simply to connect to an internal database.

You may, however, hear the term intranet misused simply to mean a local area network.

Answer 15   This is true, strictly speaking, unless the employer has obtained the employee's permission to store the data. If the employer is not registered under the Data Protection Act it should be, if it is storing this sort of information.

However it is more likely that the employee's actions would be prohibited under the organization's policy on Internet use. It is a case for disciplinary action. There is no need to record and store information about sexual preferences, simply that the employee was disciplined for downloading inappropriate material.

7 Certificate

Completion of this certificate by an authorized person shows that you have worked through all the parts of this workbook and satisfactorily completed the assessments. The certificate provides a record of what you have done that may be used for exemptions or as evidence of prior learning against other nationally certificated qualifications.

Pergamon Flexible Learning and ILM are always keen to refine and improve their products. One of the key sources of information to help this process is people who have just used the product. If you have any information or views, good or bad, please pass these on.

INSTITUTE OF LEADERSHIP & MANAGEMENT

SUPER**SERIES**

Collecting Information

....

has satisfactorily completed this workbook

Name of signatory   ....

Position   ....

Signature   ....

Date   ....

Official stamp

Fourth Edition

INSTITUTE OF LEADERSHIP & MANAGEMENT

SUPERSERIES

FOURTH EDITION

To order – phone us direct for prices and availability details
(please quote ISBNs when ordering) on 01865 888190